MW01282249

THE PROFESSIONAL GHOSTWRITER'S HANDBOOK

*LAUNCH YOUR OWN SUCCESSFUL
WRITING CAREER
BY WRITING BOOKS FOR OTHERS*

by J.S. Menefee

What People are Saying…

C.C. Sullivan
"The Ghostwriting Handbook is an enlightening and informational book which delves into the step-by-step process of learning the skills to becoming a successful ghostwriter. I truly enjoyed reading this handbook, and learned a lot from it!"

C. Daily
"It has a LOT of very good information in it! It truly is informational and an excellent guide."

Debbie Willette
"Jeremy Menefee's Professional Ghostwriting Handbook breaks down the process of ghostwriting in a methodical, easy-to-understand way, from start to finish. Perfect for writers wanting to expand their career!"

Patt O'Neil

"Have you ever wondered if you could be a Ghost Writer, or even what a Ghost Writer is? Then this is the book for you. Mr. Menefee explains the field using clear definitions and personal experience. When you read this book, it will feel like you have a mentor at your side."

Song Palmese

"Jeremy's book gives a clear and well defined path to an effective and lucrative ghostwriting career."

K.L. Holloway

"More informative than I imagined. Not only was the information useful as far as writing went, but the same ideas could be applied to marketing as an author and for writing guests posts on other blogs. Exceptional."

© **2017 Jeremy Menefee**

All rights reserved. This book or any portion thereof may not be reproduced or used in any other manner whatsoever without the express written permission of the author, except for the use of brief quotations in a book review.

Cover: Amy's Designs
(https://www.facebook.com/Amy.H.Designs/)

Editing: Dennis W. Doty
(http://www.dennisdotywebsite.com/)

Formatting: K.H. Formatting
(www.facebook.com/KHFormat)

Special thanks are due Debbie Willette, Julie Eger, and C.C. Sullivan for beta reading this book. Also, Song Palmese, Brent Harris, and Patt O'Neil. Together, these wonderful people helped to improve this book tremendously, and any remaining mistakes are the author's, not theirs. I would also like to thank "R.M., a client, for agreeing to write a forward for this book.

Visit the author's website for other works of fiction and nonfiction. The author's blog has additional free content relevant to the professional freelance writer or ghostwriter.

Freelancing Website:
http://hyperurl.co/JMenefeeFreelance
Author Web Page: http://hyperurl.co/jsmenefee
Newsletter Signup: http://smarturl.it/JSMNewsletter

You want a free ebook?
Good, because it's yours!

One last thing…

You bought my book, and so now, I want to give you a copy of another ebook!

Simply go to the URL below and follow the directions, and I'll share it with you at no cost.

Simply to thank you for your time.

Your gift…
3 Easy Outlines for Ghostwriters: Quickly ghostwrite novels that Rock!
(http://smarturl.it/3EasyOutlines_GWH)

Table of Contents

FORWARD 1

INTRODUCTION 4

WHY BE A GHOSTWRITER? 9

WHAT IS A GHOSTWRITER? 10
ETHICS OF GHOSTWRITING 11
TYPES OF GHOSTWRITING CLIENTS 13
THE GOOD AND THE BAD 16
LEVERAGE YOUR PASSIONS 21

GHOSTWRITING REQUIREMENTS 24

BENEFITS OF DEGREES 24
TAKE ONLINE COURSES 26

INTERNAL CHECKLIST 28

WRITING ABILITY 28
ONGOING LEARNING 29
OUTLINING SKILL 31
SELF-EDITING ABILITY 34
COMMUNICATIONS SKILLS 39
LETTING GO OF THE NUT 41
GHOSTWRITING MINDSET 44
ELMER FUD (FEAR, UNCERTAINTY & DOUBT) 49

EXTERNAL CHECKLIST 55

HARDWARE & SOFTWARE 55
WEBSITE 58
SOCIAL MEDIA 61
EMAIL ACCOUNT 67
GOOGLE DRIVE 69
PAYPAL ACCOUNT 71
ZOHO, FRESHBOOKS, OR HIVEAGE 72
CONTENT MILLS/WORK SITES 73

JOB CONSIDERATIONS 78

So where do you start?... 78
What if you don't like romance? 79
Then comes the paperwork 79

ON CONTRACTS... 81

Clauses 81
Letter of Understanding 84
Negotiating Terms 85
Estimating Your Writing Time 87
Figuring Out Your Deadline 90
The Revisions Clause... 91
Portfolio Clause 92
Negotiating Online or by Phone.................................. 93

WORKFLOW 95

Outline Approval... 95
The Writing Process 97
Billing Process 99
What Should I Get Paid? 103
Talking to Clients About Budget 105

Q&A: OTHER WORK QUESTIONS 107

Q: What should I do if the client offers to credit
me as co-author? 107
Q: If the contract is for 80k words but I write 87k,
what do I do? 108
Q: Can I still use the milestone payments system if I
don't want to share the content with the client
until the book is completed?...................................... 111
Q: How much input will the client have? 112
Q: What if a client is unsatisfied with the book you
write? 115
Q: What do you do if a client refuses to pay? Do you
own the writing?... 117
Q: Do you always have to sign an NDA and Non-
Compete Agreement?.. 119

Q: Do you ever get credit for your writing? 119

    Q: How do you build your portfolio if you can't
reference your work?.. 121

GETTING CLIENTS 123

Content Mills 124
Advertising.. 124
Social Media and Word of Mouth 125
Nonprofits 127
Quid Pro Quo 128

STEP-BY-STEP WORK PROCESS 130

Getting Prepared 130
Finding Clients.. 133
Getting the Contract Signed 134
Workflow Process 135
Billing 138
Conclusion 139

TAXES 141

Gather Paperwork and Receipts 141
Things to Deduct 143

CLOSING.. 145
APPENDIX: SAMPLES.. 147

Content Mill Proposal 147
Email Proposal 148
Letter of Understanding 150

ABOUT THE AUTHOR 157

Forward

Turning ideas into finished manuscripts. That's what ghostwriters do.

As a ghostwriter, you give ideas life. You allow them a chance to be seen and enjoyed by many readers. It all starts with an idea, but most of the time, it ends there. But you, as a ghostwriter, can come to the rescue. You can save the idea from being just that: an idea without execution.

About two years ago, I had what I thought was a great idea for a book. Something that was a different take on a hungry sub-genre that I had great interest in. They'd love this book, I thought. Absolutely eat it up. But I was time-starved, and therefore, execution was nil.

As a business owner who dabbled with writing in my free time, I knew my idea would remain as just as idea, forever, unless I did something. Up until that time, I wasn't too familiar with the term "ghostwriter." Sure, I knew that The Hardy Boys and Nancy Drew book series were ghostwritten, but I had no idea James Patterson used a ghostwriter to help him with his process. But I knew that without help, my great idea would shrivel up, like most great ideas before it, never seeing the light of day.

Then I went on the hunt for a ghostwriter and, after sifting through many writing samples, I found Jeremy. At that time, I had no idea what I was doing or where my idea would go, but I knew one thing: with a ghostwriter, it wouldn't be stuck in my brain any longer. Instead, it would now finally be unleashed upon the world.

I remember when I received the first few chapters from Jeremy. I was excited to see my idea coming to life. With each chapter received, it was like opening up a present. As the project progressed, it started taking on a life of its own. With Jeremy's help, different plot ideas were presented and we worked together to make the story world even more rich, the plot even more twisting and turning. The collaborative relationship we were developing was spawning off a series that wouldn't have existed if only I, a single person, was in involved in the process. *The results were magical.*

With my business knowledge and marketing ideas, I was able to focus more time on branding and promotion for the book series. Normally, self-published authors have to juggle all aspects—idea selection, outlining, writing, cover design, working with an editor, promotion, etc—but working with a ghostwriter helped me to juggle all those things and more, even with my hectic work schedule.

Not only was I able to get my idea out of my head and onto paper, but I was able to leverage my business skills and apply them to the series. I was able to grow my publishing platform quickly, even while swamped with non-publishing work. It was all made possible because I hired a ghostwriter.

To this day, I still work with Jeremy as we expand the series and plan out new books. Working with him brings me great joy and happiness, because I know that without him, my great idea would still be floating around in my head, screaming to be let loose.

As a ghostwriter, you give ideas wings, allowing them to make their way into the world to make it a more entertaining place.

R.M.

Introduction

I have been writing (including ghostwriting) and editing professionally for over twenty years. I've done a lot of ghostwriting in the tech industry, both at the start of my career and for clients of a public relations agency at which I later worked. Yet, when I first began ghostwriting novels in 2015, I had *never written fiction* except for my own enjoyment. I didn't even write for enjoyment very often because I usually had been copywriting all day already, and my creative urges were largely met through tabletop role-playing games.

My only real qualification for writing fiction, when I first began, was simply that I read a lot and always have. Sure, I had been writing for decades, but not fiction. I can now tell you that fiction is an entirely different beast. **There was definitely a learning curve.**

Here's how it all started...

Someone saw my extensive Goodreads lists and checked out my online profile, where he found out I was a writer. He didn't know I wasn't a *fiction* writer, yet. He contacted me to ask if I'd be interested in writing a novel for him. He had a great idea, but didn't write in English well enough to do it justice. The money was worth my time, and I had always been interested in writing novels, so I happily accepted his offer.

First, however, I told him that I had zero experience writing fiction professionally. He asked if I had any samples I could send, just things I'd written for myself. I sent a 5k short story about two kids surviving a plague that had effectively wiped out civilization as far as they knew. I can look at that story now and see that it's painfully bad compared to the writing I now produce, but he loved it. It was better than most of the fiction coming out these days, he said.

That's when I first got the notion of ghostwriting fiction to phase out my usual business writing.

It turns out, the quality of my first book was solid. The client was pleased. But in the long run, what was most valuable about writing that first novel wasn't a happy client. It was that I began to learn what works, what doesn't, novel structure and pacing, and so on. There are many things you learn about writing from reading books and listening to lectures, but I can safely say that there are many more things that only "click" after you've done some real fiction writing.

Essentially, he paid me to learn to write fiction well.

That's pretty darn cool, right? I now have far more experience, with over a dozen novels written in addition to my usual nonfiction, business, and other content writing. And as much as I truly do love copywriting and editing, I've discovered that fiction is my passion, whether ghostwriting or writing for myself.

Not everyone can say they truly love their job, so I consider myself pretty lucky.

Ghostwriting, as the old saying goes, is a great job if you can get the work. Everyone has heard of ghostwriting, but few ghostwriters talk about how they do it, so the field is a bit of a mystery to most. There isn't a lot of information available on the subject. Ghostwriting may sound hard, but it really isn't.

If you can write a book, you can ghostwrite. Anyone can learn to write a book well enough to be a ghostwriter.

Given what I've learned and the joy fiction writing has brought me, I was inspired to share my experiences and my methods. My long history of writing nonfiction and business materials makes me well-suited to address this topic. My more recent experience ghostwriting gives me the insights needed to show you how to do it yourself. And as anyone who knows me online and offline can attest, I love to help aspiring writers new to the field. I continually post helpful how-tos, and I answer questions online as often as I can. I believe in sharing information as widely as possible, and this book is, for me, a continuation of that philosophy.

I intend to show you exactly what to do, step by step, so that you can get started in ghostwriting. I want you to be able to earn a living doing this while you work on your own novels or pick up the skills you will need to do so. Thankfully, ghostwriting can pay the bills and make you a better writer at the same time.

Get paid to learn. Learn to write. And write for money—which you can then use to publish your own novels. They'll be good novels, too, because you'll have gained the writing experience that it takes to put out a quality manuscript with a strong story and tight plotting. With ghostwriting, all the skills you need to succeed as an author are yours for the taking, just by writing—and getting paid for it.

If you intend to become a mid-level author (at the least) who eventually earns a living through your own novels, then this is the book for you.

Why Be a Ghostwriter?

Why, indeed? For money, power, and a superyacht, of course. Okay, probably not, but it's a nice dream. I certainly don't have a yacht, and I could always use more money. You won't become obscenely rich ghostwriting, but you can make decent money with it as either a full-time job or "side gig."

With ghostwriting, a world of opportunity is accessible to everyday writers—those who *haven't* worked around celebrities for twenty years before diving into a ghostwriting career focused on high-profile memoirs.

What's your poison? If you like to write romance novels, there are clients coming out of the woodwork. Science Fiction? Those clients are out there waiting to hire you. Paranormal? Yes, they're hiring. There are clients out there for everyone, looking to hire writers in every genre.

And again… They pay you to gain experience in writing solid fiction.

What is a Ghostwriter?

A ghostwriter is a professional writer of books and other materials on which the clients are listed as the authors, even though they didn't draft it. The ghostwriter usually can't disclose what they wrote or for whom, has no rights to the material they write, and doesn't earn royalties. It's work-for-hire. You get paid to write a book, and then your involvement ends.

When people hear of ghostwriting, they often think of celebrity autobiographies where an actor or musician has their name on the cover, but everyone knows they did not write it. To be clear, the artist probably verified the material. They definitely provided the writer with the details, contacts, clippings, interviews, and so on to draft the book, but that is where their input ends. It's a not-so-secret secret in the entertainment industry.

Why would a celebrity hire someone to write their book for them? The answer is easy. Either they lack the writing experience and skill to develop an excellent book themselves (because they aren't professional writers), or they lack the time to write it but feel they need that book for marketing or career reasons.

Decision made, they hire someone with years of experience writing celebrity biographies and work closely with them throughout the process. At the end of that process, the celebrity will revise the manuscript and add their own anecdotes or "voice" to the story. The book will then be published, either listing the celebrity as the sole author or (rarely) listing the ghostwriter as the co-author.

If people have heard of ghostwriting at all, this is their common perception. But as I will explain, *there are many more kinds of ghostwriting than just celebrity memoirs*, and you will get to pick and choose what you want to write. That's a good thing, because there aren't a lot of celebrity memoir jobs to go around compared to the unending supply of contracts available for fiction and nonfiction alike.

Ethics of Ghostwriting

One commonly asked question is whether ghostwriting is unethical or dishonest. While everyone has to make this determination for themselves, I tend to think that the answer depends on the type of ghostwriting I'm doing. It also matters who is hiring me and why they need a ghostwriter.

You may decide differently than I would, and that's okay. Personal ethics are *personal*, after all.

For me, I feel that the decision of whether a gig is ethical or not is largely moot. To me, any breach of ethics is committed only by the byline… the client. The ghostwriter, in my opinion, is merely a professional writer providing a contract service. I let the client worry about the ethics of their choice to use a ghostwriter, since my name isn't on it. Neither is yours!

Look at it this way. You know that paid spokespeople are given a script to read, right? Ghostwriting is far more ethical than being paid to endorse a product you don't use. But guess what… Someone wrote that script, and they may or may not use the product. They wrote it because a customer paid them to write it.

Or how about this—news anchors read each segment from a teleprompter. Did they write that news segment? No. Someone else did. That fact is irrelevant to the quality of the news they deliver, though. It's either accurate or it isn't.

Did you know that a news editor adjusts the story submitted by field reporters and columnists? I can tell you from experience that what goes out under a reporter's name is often *not* the story the reporter submitted. Material is added or removed, and even the story angle is adjusted to meet the news outlet's tone, political stance, available space for the story, and other factors. Yet the reporter's name is still on the story in the newspaper.

My point is that, unlike spokespeople, you aren't lying. You're a professional being paid to write content, whether for a book, a blog, a website, or a novel. The fact that your client will publish it as though they wrote it has nothing to do with you. *You* are paid to *write*, not to publish. If there's some dishonesty, it's on the part of the clients. You are personally unstained by that.

Types of Ghostwriting Clients

Here is a list of the types of ghostwriting you may commonly be called to do, and some ethical considerations that may affect your decision on whether to accept a contract.

Content & Business Writing

The client is purchasing all rights to the materials, and everyone knows this going on. Because it's merely a business decision, and a business transaction, there isn't any ethical conflict here. Business is business, and you provide a professional service.

Authority Articles

Also called "contributed articles" in the marketing industry. In these cases, the client is *not* a professional writer. After you deliver the material, it's practically guaranteed that the byline, other C-level executives, the marketing department, and the PR agency will all revise it extensively. What gets published is likely to bear little resemblance to what you wrote. As with business writing, it's strictly a business transaction. I don't see any problem with this.

Fiction Novels

Three types of people hire ghostwriters for fiction novels.

- First, someone with a story burning within, striving to get out and be told—but who lacks the language or writing skills to do it justice. These people provide the outline and summaries for you to write from, or even their own rough draft to rewrite. I personally have no problem helping these people realize their dream by ghostwriting for them, but some ghostwriters don't accept fiction contracts. That's fine, too.

- Second, marketers whose profession is promoting books with their pen names on them. They usually have multiple pen names for different genres. Because it's a *business contract* to them, that's all it is to me, as well.

- Lastly, big-name authors who have more story ideas than time. They may pay large sums to have someone else write it, but they usually work closely with the ghostwriter to make sure it sounds like them and is true to their vision. This is, in my opinion, the most questionable of all the ghostwriting types. Having said that, I'm a professional. If they want to hire me, I'm available for the right price. It's the only category that makes me feel like a wordsmith mercenary, though, and it's not for everyone.

Nonfiction Books

Clients for these are either subject-matter experts who need a book for their resumé, or marketers. I have no problem writing for either category. For the subject matter expert, I tend to just think of it like a large authority article. For the marketers, it's just a business transaction. Either way, I'm not bothered by it.

The Good and the Bad

Ghostwriting does have some pros and cons. You won't get rich, but if you have the discipline to write consistently, you can make a living. A ghostwriting contract for a book-length project provides you with a dependable income. Writing a book takes quite a while, and you get paid throughout the project (or perhaps at the end of the contract—see the chapter on CONTRACTS). Generally, the total fees for ghosting a novel are higher than for most other writing projects.

What if you don't want to write full-time? Well, it's easy to make ghostwriting into just another stream of income for your freelance writing business, especially if you can type quickly and follow my advice about outlining.

Best of all, you can use ghostwriting as a stepping stone toward writing your own novels. Your contracts pay the way, and at the end of a contract or two, you can be confident that your writing is good enough to make people want to buy your books.

The stereotype of the novice writer is the person who spends several years to draft a 250,000-word monster novel. You won't make that mistake—you'll write quickly, on-target to at least a basic outline, knowing

the number of words you can write eac'
consistently.

You won't have to struggle to find cli
there are more people who want ghostwriters ...
there are people willing to do the job. For those of us
who have tuned in and realized this, there is never a
lack of work.

When you consider that many authors can't support
themselves with their writing alone, I believe that I
regularly make more from what I charged to
ghostwrite than the client made from selling the book.

How Everyone Benefits

Professional marketers, one of the core client types I
discuss in this book, make their money through
momentum and back catalog. They don't have to make
money on any one book to make more money overall
(a trick you'll learn when you study how to launch your
own novels in other books). If the client can't make
money on that one book, the residual sales of their
back catalog makes up for it. For marketer clients, it's a
numbers game.

One of these professional book marketers I spoke with
said he makes over $100,000/year in profit from
twenty books published under four pen names, all

written by professional writers. Half of those
oks made money on launch, and the other half were
slow performers," as he called them.

But he said it works out well for us both. He makes
more money on his entire catalog of books for every
unprofitable one, because it leads people to his other
books that *do* sell well. And the books I wrote for him
have gone to the Top 20 of their genres, boosting him
further.

With ghostwriting, the clients do the work I don't
want to do. I don't have to arrange and pay for cover
art. I don't have to hire an editor, because the client
will do that. I don't have to format the manuscript for
publication—they do that, too. Or they won't, but
that's okay for me because it isn't my byline on the
cover. I get paid regardless of how well the book does.

Sure, some contracts pay more than others, but I make
a living doing what I love. We all know people who
have written fantastic books, ones we've read and
loved, just to discover they've sold only a couple
hundred copies. I don't have to worry about that.

Maybe your ghosted books will become Amazon
bestsellers, as a few of mine have, but I never have to
worry about whether the book is going to be profitable
or if it will lose money—and neither will you.

Is there really plenty of work?

If you're willing to write romance novels, there's a never-ending supply of clients. I don't write romance novels because it's not a genre I read or have experience with, and I do just fine, but there's no reason for you not to try it. If you're just starting your ghostwriting career, there is a never-ending supply of romance clients!

See RESOURCES[1] for the absolute best book in the universe on how to write romance novels that sell—which means novels that clients will love, and for which they'll hire you again and again.

Get Paid to Get Good

My favorite benefit to ghostwriting novels is that, at the entry level, it might as well be a **paid writing internship**. I have mentioned this earlier, but it bears repeating. Someone else foots the bill for your writing education, and you'll learn how to structure, plot, and pace a novel and build compelling, vivid characters—all by actually doing it yourself. There is no better education than experience.

---

[1] Resources - http://smarturl.it/GWritingResources

The Flip Side

Despite my fervent wishes, ghostwriting isn't all glory and drinking cocktails on yachts. It takes a certain mindset to be able to let go of your golden words, knowing someone else will get the credit (and the royalties). Many people just aren't okay with someone else getting credit for their work. That's understandable, I suppose, but a ghostwriter must come to terms with it. **A professional writer does the job to the contract terms** and then moves on to the next one.

Another downside is that speed matters, yet you have to maintain quality even while you write faster than you ever thought possible. By the time you finish your first novel's draft, your writing speed will seem blazingly fast compared to when you started. You'll also be better able to shift and adapt the writing flow, pacing, and even plotlines on the fly as you write, which will save a metric ton of time.

When you ghostwrite you don't build a readership following. No matter how many books you write, each book stands on its own as far as you're concerned. When you write six novels for yourself, each book increases interest in all the ones before it. The ghostwriter builds only clients.

One more downside: you can't add the book to your portfolio, due to non-disclosure agreements. Clients don't want it widely known that they didn't write the thing that has their name on it. How do you get around that? I discuss that under CONTRACTS later in this book.

The Jury is in…

When you look at the benefits of this profession, it's hard to find ones better anywhere in the writing field. Steady income is uncommon with freelance writing, but readily available with ghostwriting. Nowhere else will you be paid to learn how to follow your dream and write fiction.

Because your deadline is likely to be quite distant, even though you'll need the discipline to write to a word count every day, you have the luxury of working according to your own schedule—a very nice bonus.

Leverage Your Passions

You can choose contracts to write in the genres you love. That's a very big deal, because it means you'll enjoy writing what you already like to read. It also means that you begin with considerable knowledge of the things readers expect from those genres—the tropes or cliches to avoid, elements that must be included, and so on.

My first fiction novels were a Fantasy Thriller and a Fantasy Adventure. Since that time, most of the books I have written have been in my favorite genres, Post-Apocalyptic and Dystopian adult speculative fiction. I have to search a bit harder to find contracts in genres I like, but I do find them.

But did you know that you can also find clients who want nonfiction books? Not just biographies, but how-to books and reference books on almost any topic under the sun. I've written books on AGILE-project management and on how to train your pitbull, in addition to computer and tech-focused books. It's important to know that ghostwriting opportunities abound in both nonfiction and fiction.

Because of all this, you can take your experience and your passions—the things you love to do already—and find clients looking to create books on those topics. For example, if you are an R/C plane enthusiast, there may well be someone, somewhere, looking for a ghostwriter for a book on the latest and greatest models, or how to choose the perfect R/C plane.

One of my core interests is permaculture/sustainable agriculture, and sure, I've leveraged that into my post-apocalypse novels, but I've also written two nonfiction books about it for nonprofits in Kenya, Africa. How cool is that?

There are thousands of books published on every topic you can think of. By pursuing contracts for books on topics you already know about, *you have a competitive advantage* over someone like me, who knows almost nothing about R/C planes. Could I write such a book? Absolutely. Could you do it faster and better? Quite possibly.

There aren't many professional fields in which you can literally pick and choose your job duties. With ghostwriting, however, you absolutely can, simply by pursuing the nonfiction or fiction genres that interest you personally.

Make a list of the subjects you're passionate about. Add to this list all the things you have more experience with than the average person on the street. You don't have be a master, but your existing knowledge will help you close the deal and get the contract, as well as knowing what to research instead of having to study-what-to-study. Trust me on that.

Pick and choose what you write, and get paid before the book is published… That's pretty compelling! Not to mention, fun.

Ghostwriting Requirements

There are some skills you will need. Some of these, you can learn as you go or learn by reading and studying. Others are inborn characteristics that make some people better than others when it comes to ghostwriting. With study and practice, *any writer* can become a successful ghostwriter. Let's talk about some of these factors.

Benefits of Degrees

People often ask whether a degree is necessary in order to become a ghostwriter. Quite simply, the answer is *no, you don't need a degree.*

If you ghostwrite nonfiction books, or maybe articles, the so-called "authority pieces" for clients who just need a book or published article to demonstrate expertise in their niche, then a degree related to the subject is a competitive advantage, but still not required.

As a freelance writer (remember, that's what a ghostwriter is), research and interviews with experts on the subject matter can make up for a lack of a relevant degree. I've written nonfiction books on everything from AGILE Project Management to two-factor authentication to JAVA IDE development without any relevant degrees.

On the other hand, if you're ghostwriting fiction, then a degree in English or an MFA will be a huge help, *not for the writing*, but for getting clients. The acquisitions editor at a Big 5 publisher doesn't care one tiny little bit whether you have an MFA because they know it's irrelevant and has nothing to do with writing ability, but your clients tend to be everyday people. They may be impressed by an MFA, where a more experienced professional won't be. I don't have an MFA or any degrees in English or Creative Writing, and I've done very well ghostwriting fiction and nonfiction alike.

I'll say it again: A degree isn't required to be a successful ghostwriter. It can help you to get clients, but you can also get clients without one.

Take Online Courses

It's never too late to take classes on subjects that interest you, though! There are so many free and low-cost courses you can take online that it's possible to study almost any subject that interests you. You can do an internet search for online college courses and go from there. Perhaps the most commonly known online courses providers are Coursera[2] and Udemy[3]. There are many others, so if those two don't offer what you need, then you can Google free online courses on the topic. Another more recent source of online courses might be your local library, some of which offer classes through the highly-rated Gale and Lynda.com.

Want to write Romance in historical settings? Perhaps a history course would be helpful. Victorian-era literary fiction? Find a course on Victorian culture and society. Whatever your interests, you can probably find a related course online. Some take only a few hours while others are an ongoing commitment, so in addition to finding courses to match your interests, you can find ones that match your available free time.

---

[2] Coursera - https://www.coursera.org/
[3] Udemy - https://www.udemy.com/courses/

For more hands-on subjects such as woodworking or blacksmithing, you may have more luck finding detailed information on YouTube. Whatever hands-on subject I need to research, I can always find dozens of excellent videos on YouTube that show me what to do, so that I can write it clearly.

While YouTube videos don't provide the breadth and depth of subject knowledge you'll get from a well-taught course, if you only need to know how to blacksmith a knife in an emergency situation for your novel, that is precisely the sort of thing YouTube is ideal for; you can write the scene at hand and sound like you know what you're doing.

Internal Checklist

Here is a list of skills you need to have or develop if you want to be successful in ghostwriting. If these aren't natural talents, you can learn them with practice.

Writing Ability

It's important to be honest with yourself about the level of your writing ability because you can damage your credibility by overpromising. It's hard to bounce back from that, though not impossible.

If you're just beginning, **don't despair**. Every author, past and present, has been right where you are at one point in their lives (me too!). I remember being a bit scared the first time I landed a fiction contract.

Just remember that talent and experience are not the same thing. Plenty of writers with little inborn talent have gone on to be wildly successful authors, because study and practice form the foundation of writing ability. Study and practice turn whatever initial level of talent you possess into advanced skill. Ghostwriting will give you plenty of it.

Ongoing Learning

I would suggest to you that ghostwriting—an opportunity to learn the craft on someone else's dime—should be treated a lot like a series of classes. Finish one book, integrate what you've learned, and move on to the next. The same holds true with online courses and YouTube playlists. There are many writing vlogs (video blogs) and video courses on YouTube.

Throughout your writing career, you'll continue to learn the craft and business of writing through both practice and study. What should you study? How do you gain practice and experience? Both answers are simple, yet difficult.

Online Study

First, I'd say you should study other writers. Then, you should also think about joining Facebook writing-focused groups. Not just any groups, though. Yes, join one or two groups aimed at beginners such as *Where Authors Begin*[4], but you'll also want to join and

---

[4] Where Authors Begin -
https://www.facebook.com/groups/516756898457588/

participate in some groups aimed at more advanced writing. I've listed some great groups under RESOURCES[5].

Book Larnin'

Read and read some more. In my opinion, as a professional writer you should always be reading one novel in your chosen genre or genres and one book on the profession or craft of writing. Even if you only read one chapter each day, how-to books such as those listed under RESOURCES are your lifeline to quickly improving your writing.

If you go to Amazon to look for books on the writing craft, you will likely be overwhelmed. There are thousands on the subject—some good, most mediocre. The best starter books[5] by far are:

- *Outlining Your Novel*, K.M. Weiland

- *Structuring Your Novel*, K.M. Weiland

- *The 12 Key Pillars of Novel Construction*, C.S. Lakin

If you read only three books on writing, these are the ones I'd strongly recommend because they form the

---

[5] Best starter books - http://smarturl.it/GWritingResources

foundation of all the writing you'll do. Even if you only read these books once, you'll understand how to build the framework for your novels and the actual writing will come to you quickly.

Study these and other books as though your career depends upon it. In truth, it does. *Never stop reading about the craft.* I've been writing for decades, yet I still read books on the writer's craft. Many are still basic-level books, because refresher courses are just as important as new information. I often pick up tips and tricks I hadn't considered, or had taken for granted and not considered thoroughly, even in books about basic writing techniques.

Outlining Skill

You may sense that I'm a fan of outlining. I would suggest that, for a ghostwriter, **outlining is the single most important thing you can do** to write better, faster. The faster you write, the faster you get paid to write. *Speed is money.*

Typing speed will improve on its own as you get used to writing (if you currently struggle with that), but nothing will ever improve your ability to quickly structure and write a novel like a simple outline will.

For some people, outlining is a long, drawn-out process that ends with the novel half-written already. The Snowflake Method[6] is an excellent example of this outlining style. It doesn't work for me, but it might be a blessing to you. Try it!

For other writers, an outline might be nothing more complicated than a bullet list of chapters, each having one sentence giving the overview of what happens in that chapter.

Most of us fall somewhere between. We generate the basic characters with their strengths, flaws, goals, and conflicts. We might write a paragraph for each scene, detailing who is involved, the POV character's objective, the obstacle, and the outcome. We might tag scenes by their relevant plot or subplot so we can better control pacing (J.K. Rowling is famous among writers for this).

Gold Standard in Outlining Apps

The "magic bullet" for outlining and/or plot gridding quickly and effectively is an amazing free online tool

---

[6] Snowflake Method - http://www.advancedfictionwriting.com/articles/snowflake-method/

called Hiveword[7]. If you get hired to write a complex book or a trilogy, this tool is a lifesaver.

You can do the same level of work, however, with a spreadsheet or separate Word document, or with the outlining tool included in your favorite writing suite. Heck, some authors just use a sheet of paper and a pencil. It's important to have one process and become familiar with it, whatever process you choose. Obviously, I recommend Hiveword, but if you have another system already, there's nothing wrong with using that.

I have a great post about how to use Hiveword on my blog[8].

The Purpose of Outlining

Remember, it's not about what you *like*, but about what helps you to write a better book faster. For me, that means medium-detail writeups for each character, chapter summaries, scene summaries, and a plot grid[9] to help me make sure every subplot gets regular loving

---

[7] Hiveword - http://www.hiveword.com/

[8] How to Use Hiveword - https://jmenefeeblog.wordpress.com/2016/11/29/perfect-integrated-writing-tools/

[9] Plot Grid - http://smarturl.it/GWritingResources

attention. You won't know what works for you until you try them out.

Whatever the outline level, whatever tool you use to make it, one thing nearly all successful ghostwriters have in common is a willingness to outline before writing. If you haven't outlined before, then learn. Once you've done it once or twice, it will become second nature and you'll wonder how you got by without it, particularly when you need to write a book under a tight deadline.

Self-Editing Ability

Another key to being a good ghostwriter—one who gets repeat business and word-of-mouth clients—is the ability to turn in solid writing. Save revisions and corrections for later, at the edit stage. While you're writing, just write. Don't edit! This will increase your writing speed by a surprising amount. Begin editing when you're finished drafting.

Self-editing is a skill anyone can learn to do well enough for ghostwriting. Obviously, nothing beats having your own editor, because I guarantee they'll find hundreds of things to fix or improve within every chapter. They come at it with fresh eyes and vast experience with editing that you aren't likely to have.

But when you're ghostwriting, you don't have an editor. Why spend your money on an editor for a book that isn't in your name, and for which the client will hire an editor anyway? But it's important that you learn editing basics. You need to submit a MSS (manuscript) that is as close to publication-ready as you can. You want the client to come back for more, and that means giving them a professional level of work.

How do you learn to self-edit? First, by reading. I recommend these books: *EDITING the RedPen Way* by Anne Rainbow as a good starting point. Another excellent book on how to self-edit is *Self Editing for Fiction Writers* by Renni Brown and Dave King.

Second, create a checklist of things to look for. You may need to re-read your work multiple times, each cycle looking for a specific item, but with time you'll become more efficient.

The absolute top things to look for when ghostwriting fiction include:

- **Consistent Tense** - if you write the book in past tense, you have to ensure you don't switch to present tense in places. It's easy to accidentally write, "I go to the market, but I felt sad about my conversation with Mom," and then simply not see it when you re-read and edit. *Pay attention to that.* Nothing marks an amateur faster than tense changes.

- **Single POV** - Every scene must only be from *one* character's viewpoint. You cannot include Frank's feelings if the scene is written from Tom's POV. "Tom glowered at Frank, feeling enraged, but Frank just didn't care." No! Tom doesn't know what Frank cares about. Instead, you'd write something like "Tom glowered at Frank, feeling enraged, but Frank showed no reaction." It's a subtle but important difference.

- **Use One Font** - Always write in either Times New Roman or Courier New, with a font size of 12pt. Make sure it's the same font and size throughout. The easiest way of doing that is to highlight everything (control-A) and then select your font and font size. This will make everything consistent. Update "normal" text to match. Note that you *can* use a different font for things within the novel like showing a letter written by or to a character, but be consistent there, too.

- **No Spaces After Paragraphs** - Make sure your writing software isn't adding a space between paragraphs, and that you aren't hitting Enter twice. It's best not to use a tab at the beginning of each paragraph, either. The best way is to use your writing software's ruler to adjust each paragraph's starting location. The Help section of your writing tool or program will have information on how to do this.

- **Spell Check Everything** - Duh! Sounds easy, but you'd be surprised at how many people's MSS I edit that have simple typos. Clients hate them even more than editors, because it proves you don't care and couldn't be bothered to do the basics. If they find a lot of typos, how good can the rest of the writing be?

- **Break Up Long Paragraphs** - Especially in dialogue, long paragraphs are daunting and readers (including your client) tend not to like them.

  - No paragraph should be longer than 6-8 lines, with only a few exceptions in the entire book.

  - Dialogue should be short and punchy, no longer than 3-5 lines before someone else responds, does something, or thinks something.

Once you're done with that, run it through HemingwayApp[10] or Grammarly[11] to catch punctuation errors. Try to revise any sentence that the app labels as being too complex. A few complex sentences are fine—you don't *want* all your lines simple and short, regardless of the advice you may sometimes hear online, but no more than one or two complex sentences per page.

Grammar applications may also try to tell you the basic reading level of your book. I've heard some misinformed people say writing shouldn't exceed a 3rd-grade reading level, but I disagree. Unless it's middle-grade fiction, anything between 5th and 7th grade is fine. You want to avoid going higher than that to keep from confusing the readers, and you don't want to be lower than that or most readers will be bored to tears. It's best if your writing is neither confusing nor boring.

Let me give you a tip about using grammar applications: *they're often wrong*. If your gut tells you not to change a word or a punctuation mark, strongly consider leaving it alone. As an editor, I can't begin to guess at how many times I've seen all these applications give bad *or even wrong* advice. However,

---

[10] HemingwayApp - http://www.hemingwayapp.com/

[11] Grammarly - https://www.grammarly.com/

until you reach a level where your self-editing is very good, those applications can make a world of difference in your writing quality. Just approach it with a grain of salt, use your judgment for each suggested change, and you'll be fine.

Communications Skills

As a writer, you're probably used to operating in a vacuum with little outside input until the novel is drafted (if ever). As a ghostwriter, however, you must communicate with your client. You should never let a week go by without at least sending them a status update, letting them know you're on target and things are going well.

I communicate frequently. I share my outline with them before writing, so they give me the go-ahead and agree with the story I intend to write. If they have different expectations, you want to find out *before* you've spent hundreds of hours writing the novel.

I also break up my manuscript into chapters, creating a different file for each. Why do I go through the trouble? Because after I've drafted a chapter, I let it sit for a few days before self-editing it. After letting a chapter "rest," a writer gains some perspective and tends to find needed edits more readily. I can then send individual chapters to the client for feedback, instead of waiting until the end. They *love it* when you consult them often, and it's part of providing customer service that exceeds their expectations.

Also, the client often has fantastic ideas I would never have thought of on my own. I ask them to make changes with Track Changes on and add as many Comments as they'd like, then return the file to me. I often get great ideas from those changes, suggestions, and comments.

Just as importantly, if your client has a problem with a chapter, you discover it early instead of at the end. At most, you may have to adjust a couple of following chapters. This process works a lot better and faster than learning about problems at the end and having to revise half the novel.

I once had a character wander off into the sunset at about the 25% mark in a novel. My intention was to leave them as a loose thread in case I got to write a sequel. Later in that novel, I forgot the character had left. It turns out, they ended up being instrumental in the next chapter. To my deep embarrassment, the client pointed it out right away, and I only had to revise one chapter.

By the way, that client went on to hire me for another novel because he loved how well I collaborated with him.

Letting Go of the Nut

The inability to write a novel quickly is the main reason people quit working as ghostwriters. As I've explained in detail earlier, speed is your friend, and outlining will solve most or all of that issue.

The next most common reason people quit ghostwriting is simply this: people sometimes can't "let go of the nut." In the '80s, I saw a documentary about a tribe in either Africa or South America (I can't remember which) who hunted a lot of monkeys. It was a staple of their diet, but they didn't go out hunting for monkeys, wasting their time trying to catch prey that was better suited to the jungle than the hunters themselves.

Instead, the hunter would find or make a burrow in a tree, wider on the inside than at the entryway. Inside, they'd place a nut. Their favorite prey would eventually come along and find the nut, stick their monkey hands into the hole, and grab it. Unfortunately for the monkey, who would hoot and holler and struggle, they couldn't get their full, closed fist out while holding the nut. Instead of letting go of the nut, the monkey stayed in their predicament, struggling but getting nowhere. The hunter would check the trap at his leisure and find the monkey. Dinner served.

Aspiring ghostwriters can easily be that monkey. The nut, of course, is the writer's golden words. Maybe they follow up incessantly with the client to find out when it will be published. Or perhaps they follow up a week after sending the finished manuscript, suggesting changes that should have been made *before* the client started prepping the book for publication.

They just can't get used to the idea that once they send the manuscript, their job is done. They don't own the words. They don't get credit on the cover and they get no byline. They can't talk about their amazing creation with their friends and family. They can't post lines of it to their favorite Facebook group on "#FFF first line Friday."

They just can't let go of the nut.

The proper mindset—the view of a *professional* ghostwriter—is that those were words-for-hire, no different than writing a blog post for a client or designing someone's book cover. You write it and you're done. Move on to the next project.

It is true that some people will never get past this hangup, never be comfortable knowing that someone else's *Top 100 All Paid Ebooks* novel has nothing to do with them anymore. Even those of us who do this for a living will have those moments, I promise you. But you *can* get over it, and you can learn to let it go.

And just remember that a large majority of clients probably lose money on the book, yet you got paid. You knew in advance how much you'd be paid, and when. On average, you've probably come out even or ahead in terms of profit, Whether the book gets five sales or five thousand.

You also got paid for the book before the client did, because you earn the money up front, not from royalties. No waiting, no worrying, no nail-biting evenings spent checking the Amazon Sales Rank like a hypercaffeinated ferret. You wrote it, cashed the check, and moved on.

There's a lot to be said for that kind of security, especially in the field of freelance writing. And when you do get around to writing your own novels, you'll have all that experience. You will be far ahead of the pack on this learning curve. Don't let your lack of experience stop you from being a ghostwriter. You are on a learning curve and will improve over time.

In the meantime, you will be paid to learn and you won't damage your credibility because your name isn't on the book. Someone else got it, *had it edited to improve it*, and published it. Better yet, they're probably in the category of clients who are primarily marketers, so they won't even notice, much less care. For them, sending it to an editor is part of the process, just another regular business expense.

Ghostwriting Mindset

Despite all I've said about ghostwriting being paid training, there is a certain mindset that a ghostwriter needs to cultivate in order to be successful. In essence, it boils down to *professionalism.* As a ghostwriter, you're a professional writer. Your mentality should reflect this.

Professional writers follow certain guidelines. Here are a few of these practices:

- A professional **must** remember at all times that the client isn't necessarily a professional, themselves. They may behave unprofessionally, but there is never an excuse for you to do the same. I've had clients who didn't behave professionally, and though they were hard to work with, I received a glowing review from them because I remained the consummate professional. Take this advice to heart.

- A professional **must not** quit the job before it's completed, regardless of whether the client is a joy or a burden. If they're a bad client, simply don't work with them again. However, they must never get the idea that you think poorly of them—even your most difficult client can give you a referral that lands that dream contract.

- A professional **must** remember that the book belongs to the client, not the writer. If the client wants you to do something stupid, politely explain what you feel is the better way—and then *do what the client says.* Even if they want to begin their novel with "It was a dark and stormy night," they've hired you to write the book they want. They're paying you. It isn't personal—it's just business.

- A professional **must not** miss a deadline. If you're going to miss one, let them know ahead of time, say why, and then tell them what you will do to ensure it doesn't happen again. If you don't tell them ahead of time, then you aren't acting professionally.

- A professional **must** underpromise and overdeliver. If you think the book will take six weeks to write, tell the client it will take eight. If you promise 50k words, deliver 52k, even if you won't be paid for the extra 2k words. In real life, things come up that could delay you, but if you build in some leeway into your proposal as I suggest under FIGURING OUT YOUR DEADLINE, you still can meet your obligations. And by delivering more than they expected, you can be sure they'll use you again and possibly act as a professional reference.

- A professional **must not** annoy the client with questions and details while writing the book. Get the information you need *before* work begins. Once you start writing, every communication with the client should be about the status, and should meet or exceed their expectations.

- A professional **must** bill the client according to the terms of the contract. Don't let it slide—it'll bite you in the behind. If you agree to bill them at every 10% mark, do it the very day you reach that milestone.

- A professional **must not** work for free. Your contract should spell out any extra work you're willing to do, such as one revision per milestone or chapter (not per project), in which you will revise up to 25% of the word count. For example, in a 10k-word milestone, 2,500 words can be re-edited for free, one time. I guarantee you that you'll eventually get such a client, one who wants hour-long conference calls every day that aren't included in the contract. If your client wants more than this 25% one-time revision for free, say no. Communicate your message politely and professionally, but say no. If you first begin working for free for a client, he or she will find a never-ending list of extra things for you to do, and you'll have a hard time declining because you've already set the tone for the relationship.

- A professional **must** know what they're willing to write, and stick to that. If you don't feel comfortable writing snuff porn, then accepting such a contract will result in inferior, unenthusiastic writing. Writing is your job, not theirs, and poor writing will haunt you when you ask for a reference. It's better to miss out on a project than to take one you instinctively *know* will not be successful.

- A professional **must not** let clients know when they're stressed out or what their personal issues are. Never snap at a client because they're being difficult, *ever.* If you have to wait 24 hours before replying so you can do it calmly, then wait. Never let the client know you have human problems like everyone else. It's *never* okay, for example, to ask for an extension on a deadline because your girlfriend or boyfriend broke up with you and is moving out. Instead, see above about meeting deadlines and what to do if you'll miss one. Keep it professional, which means keeping a professional distance between you and your client.

- A professional **must never** miss a deadline. Put extra time into your contracts, instead. Then, if nothing goes wrong, you turn it in early and look good. That's much better than missing deadlines, which will almost guarantee you don't get anymore work from them or any prospective clients they know. Missing deadlines means you can forget about a good referral.

The mindset of a ghostwriter should be that of a professional writer. Even if you're working on your first book for your very first client, clients shouldn't feel that you're an amateur or unprofessional. Keep communications formal, meet your deadlines, and underpromise/overdeliver. Do this, and you will have happy customers who are glad to give you a referral and maybe even a testimonial for your web site.

Elmer FUD
(Fear, Uncertainty & Doubt)

Elmer is an aspiring writer, and he has decided to use ghostwriting as paid training before publishing his own novels, just as I've suggested. He's excited about the idea of writing, of getting paid to take what amounts to an intensive writing class. He tells his wife, his sister, and his neighbor Jim. His wife and sister are supportive, but not really enthusiastic.

Neighbor Jim, however, laughs at him and asks what makes him think he can write a novel. Has he ever taken a writing class? Has he ever written anything longer than a few short stories? Hell, has he ever read a book on writing? Jim tells him he doesn't know anything about writing, and says he's going to FAIL.

Because Jim is right about Elmer's level of experience, he thinks maybe Jim is right about the failure part, too. Everyone has fear, uncertainty, and doubt, but few things can incubate FUD more than the idea of becoming a writer.

Fortunately for Elmer, his sister points out some facts that make him feel a lot better about his idea. For one, she reminds him that he picked ghostwriting precisely *because* he has no experience as an author. By taking low-paying work through a content mill, he'll gain the experience he needs to move up and charge more.

She also points out that the book he's reading, *The Professional Ghostwriter's Handbook*, lists every step he has to take to get started. If he has a question, there are examples and links at the back he can follow, and it gives him a list of books he could read to speed up the learning process.

Then she delivers the clincher. She reminds him that of all the people who write novels successfully (however they define success), only a tiny fraction of them have degrees in creative writing, or even in English.

Sure, those people with degrees might have an easier time, and might be able to skip a few books on the reading list, but creative writing is as much art as science. Lots of people spent thousands to get a Master of Fine Arts in Creative Writing (also called an MFA) and still can't put a compelling story together.

His sister tells him her opinion that many MFAs have a harder time becoming successful authors. Not because they lack talent, nor because a degree is a bad thing, but because they may feel their education and learning are finished. Also, their instructor's primary qualification to teach was *probably* that they, too, paid thousands for a degree. She tells Elmer that in her experience, the MFA graduate may feel they have nothing left to learn—when in fact, the degree is the start of the journey, not the destination. It's understandable because people like to feel as though they've made it to the top, but being unwilling to learn is an anchor that can hold people back.

Elmer, however, is eager to learn. He knows he's going to make mistakes, he knows he'll learn from those mistakes, and he knows that people are going to pay him to make those mistakes. At the entry level on the word mills, the clients don't expect perfect prose, only fast production so they can churn out fifty novels this year under four different pen names.

His sister wisely suggests that if the client gets what they want, and Elmer learns to master this new craft he wants to pursue, isn't that a "win-win" situation?

Elmer thinks so, and I do too.

Defeating FUD

There are three traits that kill FUD fast:

1. Misplaced pride and foolish ego

2. Experience

3. Knowledge

I don't recommend the ego route. The best writers know without a doubt that they'll be better writers next year than they were last year. They know there are better writers, and that's okay because there is plenty of room for more than one style of writing.

Experience is King...

Experience breeds confidence because it increases knowledge. FUD loves the unknown. Nothing breeds FUD like something new—territory that has never been explored before. Through experience, you learn what to expect, and how to do what is expected of you.

But Knowledge is Power

Knowledge eliminates FUD precisely because it reduces the unknown and lets you gain more experience faster.

Read the books I recommend at the end of this guide, and you'll gain the knowledge you need to excel. While you can't get experience until you begin to write, you can get all the *knowledge* you want or need before you ever set pen to paper. I recommend reading one or more of my recommendations before you begin, just so you have a rough baseline of knowledge to work with.

Or you could do it as I did, and read a lot while you are writing your first books. I'd been a business writer and copywriter for a long time before I tried fiction, so I had confidence born of experience (and a bit of pride).

You may not have that experience writing other things, but you *can* read a book on the craft.

You are in Good Company

Each person who has ever become a famous author was once exactly where you are. They conquered their FUD and wrote. And kept writing. And then, one day, they realized how good they'd become. Yet, I almost guarantee that most of them *still* feel some FUD. It's normal! Writing is soul-baring in ways that non-writers will never understand, but you soon will! Because of that, however, finishing a novel is just about the biggest high you'll ever get. Nothing else really compares, except maybe BASE jumping. (I wouldn't know, since I don't jump off perfectly good buildings.)

You Can Do Better Than Me

My first novel took me exactly eight weeks to write and revise with only 60,000 words, working my butt off eight hours per day, every day. Twelve novels later, I can write a 120,000-word first draft, self-edit it, and deliver it to my client in 8 weeks *without working very hard*. Could I do that with my first novel? Heck no!

You will do a lot better than I did on your first time out. One author I know wrote 250 words per week for seven years. If you're an *author* and that's all the time you have, then by all means do what it takes to write that novel. But a *ghostwriter* doesn't have that kind of time. You'll learn to write quickly, trust me. It will come naturally.

Later, in the chapter on FIGURING OUT YOUR DEADLINE, you will find all the tools you need to figure out the *exact* length of time needed to write the book, so you never have to worry about missing a deadline. You'll only have to worry about writing X words per day, and X will be something reasonable for you. You can have confidence that you absolutely will be able to finish the novel by the deadline.

Let that knowledge rid you of your FUD.

External Checklist

Then there are the things you need that aren't inherent to you personally—things to buy, tools to use, apps to utilize, profiles you must have—that you'll need to set up *before* you begin looking for clients.

Hardware & Software

Obviously, you'll need a computer, preferably Windows-based. I use a fancy Chromebook for 99% of what I do, but that extra 1% makes it worthwhile to own a Windows-based computer even if it's old, outdated, and cranky. I don't use it, but if I need it, I have it.

I recommend having access to Microsoft Office. I've found that 99% of the time you won't need it, but for that 1%, there's no substitute. Still, you really can do this without Windows and without Office. It'll just occasionally be a pain in the rump, if you don't.

I strongly recommend a high-quality mousepad and a wrist pad. These will save wear and tear on your tendons, believe me.

For communicating with your clients, you'll want a web camera and a good USB headset with built-in microphone, as well as a cell phone. Alternatively, you can set yourself up with decent speakers, a USB microphone, and a quiet room—also useful for other kinds of work, such as creating demos or narrating.

You'll want a printer so you can print contracts, drafts, etc. Some people print a lot, but I almost never use my printer. Still, when you need it, *you really need it.* You can pick up a cheap printer, some of which are only around $20. I recommend an all-in-one printer that also has a scanner and fax machine. I've used all those features, and my all-in-one printer cost about $50.

You'll spend hours each day at the computer, so a good ergonomic chair is important. You'll regret it if you don't have one, so make this a high priority on your list of things to buy.

A large monitor saves you from eye strain. You don't need it, but you'll be grateful if you invest in one.

Get a few USB drives or SD cards (depending on your computer's ports) to back up your work. Nothing—and

I mean *nothing*—sucks more than losing a book when you're halfway through the rough draft. Believe me.

You might check out novel-writing software. The two best, hands down, are Scrivener[12] and Bibisco[13]. Neither will work on a Chromebook (unless you can set your Chromebook to dual-boot with Linux), and if you only use Word or Doc files, you won't need this kind of software.

Still, for some people, it's convenient to have everything in one application. Both Scrivener and Bibisco are *fantastic* programs. Scrivener costs about $40 and Bibisco is free. Scrivener is prettier, but they have mostly the same functions. Both do outlining, scene development, character storage, and more. Take the time to check them out.

Hiveword is an online application that has all the same features as Scrivener and Bibisco, except it has no writing environment. So if you use Word or Google Docs, as I do, then you can just get a free account at Hiveword. You'll be golden.

---

[12] Scrivener - https://www.literatureandlatte.com/scrivener.php
[13] Bibisco - http://bibisco.com/

Website

You'll need a professional-looking site just to be credible. I recommend Wordpress[14] (the free version is fine) or WIX[15]. If you use Wordpress, be sure to make your landing page a static page[16], which you can do by changing settings. This is important so that your landing page (the page visitors see when they go to your URL) can contain the right keywords and also show content that inspires prospective clients to look at the rest of your site.

Instead of showing your latest blog posts, you want it to show your basic sales pitch. Who are you? Who should consider hiring your services? What's your vision?

> **TIP:** To learn how to set your WordPress site to have a static front page, and how to set up a blog page afterward if you wish, visit WordPress's help center.

---

[14] Wordpress - https://www.wordpress.com

[15] WIX - https://www.wix.com/

[16] Static front page - https://codex.wordpress.org/Creating_a_Static_Front_Page

It should have an About page that describes you, the benefit to a client in hiring you, your experience, and your qualifications. I would include your Mission Statement, if you have one. The page doesn't need to be lengthy, and the tone should be about 70% professional, 30% personal.

On the other hand, if you're just beginning, you won't have some of that information. In that case, talk about your love of books, how much you enjoy writing, and how your client will benefit from hiring you. You aren't only marketable because of your experience! People will hire you for your enthusiasm and dedication, as well.

Notice that I listed "benefits to the client" *twice*. Ultimately, that's all your client cares about. The rest is additional information, there to convince them emotionally and logically that you're a solid choice.

Your site should have a page that discusses your rates and how you prefer to work (while also saying you are flexible). Do you offer package deals? Mention them here. What's your hourly rate? What's your per-word rate for different types of ghostwriting? You probably don't need to discuss payment methods, due dates, what tools you use to write, and other workflow-related items.

Lastly, a contact page is needed so they can… you know… contact you. Email, social media profiles, and possibly phone (if you don't mind taking calls during dinner) should all be listed.

As you get clients, you may want to add a page that includes previous clients' testimonials. It's fine if they don't want you to post their name or book title, or if they want you to use only their real name instead of their pen name, or just an acronym. Whatever way they wish to be attributed, it's important to get testimonials because third-party verification is going to boost your rates and marketability, especially after you've had a couple clients who are willing to validate your statements.

Be sure you connect all your social media accounts to your site, so that if you include a blog, the blog posts will go out to all the other platforms automatically. Every web site platform has a different method of connecting social media, so I won't include an overview of the process, but you can easily find out how to auto-post from your blog to each social media account through the site's Help files or forums.

Social media

There are several social media accounts you simply must have in order to be credible. And, you'll have to use them! Later, I'll get into easy ways to do that, almost on autopilot.

You'll also want to go to Fiverr[17] and spend some money on getting a profile pic and banner/cover image that is the same for each platform, but tailored to the size requirements of each. Most Fiverr designers will be happy to do one great cover image or banner at full price, then cheaply convert it to the other platforms, so you don't pay full price for each version. You'll have to do them all at once to get that steep discount. Expect to pay $20-$50 for this. It's very worthwhile, especially considering how little this service costs.

I paid $40 to get covers/banners for my website/blog, Twitter, Facebook Page, and MailChimp newsletters, along with a nice logo. I used *Amy's Designs[18]*, and I loved her work.

---

[17] Fiverr - http://tracking.fiverr.com/SH51r

[18] Amy's Designs - https://amyshunter.wixsite.com/amysdesigns

Twitter

Set up a Twitter account dedicated only to your writing business. Mine is @JeremyJMenefee, for example. Don't use only your name as I did, though. Instead, use something that sounds professional. I would have been better served by a Twitter name like @JMenefeeWrites or @FreelancerJSM. Definitely do NOT use something inappropriate like @daveathome420.

There are several strategies to grow your Twitter platform, but for now you don't have to do a darn thing with it except make the new account, set up your profile, and create a few Twitter Lists.

Set up your profile to sound professional but friendly. Twitter isn't your resumé, but it will be a very important platform for connecting with people and validating who you are.

Set up Twitter Lists from inside Twitter. When you find interesting posts, add them to that List with a free tool called ListBuilder[19]. The people will see that you added them to a group called "Might Need a Ghostwriter," and so this is essentially a free

---

[19] ListBuilder for Twitter - https://goo.gl/3D26m5

advertisement that goes directly to the people most likely to want your services.

Tumblr

Create a Tumblr account only if you will be posting to a blog on your web site. If so, then Tumblr is another place to which WordPress can be set up to auto-post. If you don't think you will blog, then don't bother, unless you're in love with using Tumblr.

LinkedIn

You will rarely get a client from LinkedIn. So why is it worth the hassle? Simply because clients *will* check your LinkedIn profile to validate your claims and your qualifications.

Consider LinkedIn as being nothing more than your online resumé. Complete all the sections to the best of your ability, making sure the tone is just like what you might use during a job interview.

G+

Set up a Google Plus account. For your bio space, use the same information you used in LinkedIn. There are a few books out there on getting the most out of G+, but for now you only need to have created the profile.

If you already have a personal G+ account, then you can make the G+ equivalent of a Facebook Page, instead.

Facebook

The Big Daddy of social media, no matter what people might say about it slipping in popularity. I promise you that time spent on Facebook is better spent than time on any other platform. I've had almost as many clients from Facebook as I have from word of mouth!

If you already have a Facebook account, which you probably do, then *either* set up a new account that is specific to you as a ghostwriter ("ghostwriterBob," for example) *or* simply create a Facebook Page. Whichever way you go, use your LinkedIn bio as a source for filling out your Facebook profile or page.

Remember the Groups I mentioned above? Sign up to those. Other Groups are listed under RESOURCES[20]. Spend time in those groups. *Listen and learn.* Answer questions you are absolutely certain you know the answers to, but otherwise just read and thumbs-up.

Most Groups have a thread for self-promotion, so after you've been a bit active in the group for a week or two,

---

[20] Resources - http://smarturl.it/GWritingResources

then post your self-promotion post where the rules say to.

Under settings, you can set your new Facebook profile or page to *automatically re-post* your posts to everything else, especially Twitter. If you use Buffer, then you don't want to do that because Buffer does it better. Otherwise, it's an easy step to increase your discoverability.

Buffer

Buffer[21] is an application that lets you take posts you find anywhere else and… buffer them. The application will then send the post out later, to *many* other social media platforms, at the *best time possible*. As you cruise Facebook or whatever, when you find a post you want to share (one that helps build your professional profile), simply click the Buffer button instead of Share Now. It's truly a magical app, and with it, you can deliver good content to all your profiles with hardly any effort at all.

Other Apps

If you want to expand your social media reach a bit more, here are some other great applications to use:

---

[21] Buffer - https://buffer.com

- Commun.it[22] - A great tool for Twitter management

- CrowdFire[23]- Another good tool for Twitter management

- HootSuite[24] - Lets you find compelling content and deliver it to your platforms

- TweetDeck[25] - The A+ application for Twitter management, used in addition to the above apps

- If This, Then That[26] - Works with multiple social media, blog, and site platforms

- Pinterest[27] with BoardBooster[28] and ViralWoot[29] applications

You may not see the value of Twitter, but I promise you that it comes in second only to Facebook in terms of value to you as a professional writer.

---

[22] Commun.it - https://commun.it/

[23] CrowdFire - https://web.crowdfireapp.com

[24] HootSuite - https://hootsuite.com/

[25] TweetDeck - https://tweetdeck.twitter.com/

[26] IFTTT - https://ifttt.com/

[27] Pinterest - https://www.pinterest.com/

[28] BoardBooster - https://boardbooster.com

[29] ViralWoot - https://viralwoot.com/

Email account

If you've purchased your own domain name to host your Wordpress or other site and blog, the domain should come with an email. You can definitely use that.

If, like me, you don't purchase a domain, preferring instead to use the free options, then simply get a new gmail account dedicated to your professional writing. You can forward it to your main gmail, but I recommend keeping it separate and checking it at least once daily. There are Chrome apps available at the Google Store that monitor your gmail accounts, too, so you won't miss an important email.

Note: *You can auto-forward emails from your author email address to your personal one, so you don't have to separately monitor it. In* Settings*, you can even set things up to let you reply/send from your professional email address when signed in on your personal account!*

Always use this new email address for all communications having to do with your writing business. Keep personal and work addresses separate. (I wish I'd known that when I began.)

Signature

Search for Google Chrome's app called WiseStamp[30]. With this, you can create a phenomenal signature block, complete with live links to all your social media. It tells the world you are a real, honest-to-goodness professional. The example looks like this:

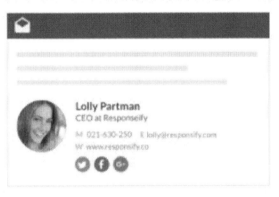

Mine is very similar, but customized. These days, there's no reason not to create your own signature block that gets appended to every email. If you have

---

[30] WiseStamp - https://www.wisestamp.com/

the skills to make it look better than WiseStamp's, by all means knock yourself out. It can never look too good.

Google Drive

This comes free with every gmail account. You get gigs of storage, *free*. Better yet, if your files are in Google Docs format, they don't count against your storage limit.

Google Drive is accessible from any of your devices. It automatically saves as you write, so you will never lose work again. And, if you drag a Microsoft Word or OpenOffice file into your drive, it auto-converts to Google Docs format. If you right-click a file in your Drive and click "download," it automatically converts it to Microsoft Word format before downloading.

I do all my writing in Drive using the Google Docs format. When I send it to the client, I download it and send the downloaded file, which has now been converted automatically to Word.

And it's secure. It isn't likely to ever get hacked, unlike some other online storage tools. Plus, you can share a link with clients to any file or folder. They might prefer the Google Docs format, which has many advantages and will also allow them to suggest changes to your manuscripts.

Most clients prefer Word via email, though, and Google Drive with Docs handles this nicely via downloading and emailing. I try to avoid using email attachments because the best part of using Google Docs is that you don't ever have to worry about "version control issues." Using Google Docs allows the client and you to access, write, or suggest changes without having to use email attachments. When you email MS Word versions to the client, they may miss an update and then make edits to an older version (or you might), leading to confusion and frustration. I cannot tell you how many hours of work I have lost to that before Google Drive came along.

There are times when a heavy edit with track changes will work better in Word than Docs, so it's still handy to have access to Word if you need it on occasion.

Template docs

In my Google Drive, I have two template files. One is for Times New Roman, and the other for Courier New. They have fonts, headings, margins, and so on all set up for me. When I begin a new project, I simply copy the template I want to use, rename the copy to the new project's title, and then start writing.

For example, my "NovelTemplate-TNR12" file creates a copy called "Copy-NovelTemplate-TNR12," which I'd then rename to "NameOfBook-Chapter1-v1." You'll find your own system.

PayPal Account

If you don't already have PayPal, set up an account. Not only does it make invoicing and receiving money easy, it separates your personal funds from business funds and provides tax documentation, which is important for TAXES, as I describe later.

If you set up a project with milestone payments, PayPal allows you to invoice the *full amount*, but click the "allow partial payments" button, and set the minimum payment to whatever fraction is reflected in the client milestone agreement in your contract. For example, if you have a 100k-word book gig and ten milestones, you'd set the minimum payment at 10% of the total.

Also, it's easy to get a PayPal debit card[31]. With that, you have access to your money right away for regular in-store purchases, without waiting 1-3 days for your

---

[31] PayPal Debit Card - http://smarturl.it/GWritingResources

bank to release it through funds transfers. That's rather nice.

Oh, and PayPal lets clients pay you a bonus if they wish, on top of the billed amount. Roughly 10% of my ghostwriting income is from performance bonuses.

Zoho, Freshbooks, or Hiveage

This step isn't strictly necessary, as I normally use Drive and Paypal alone. However, I have some business writing clients that use Zoho[32], Freshbooks[33], or Hiveage[34], so I have accounts with them and have become familiar with their many benefits.

Each of these workflow apps has tabs for documents, comments, hours worked (if you're on a gig that pays hourly), and more. They allow billing and invoicing through PayPal, but from within the application. Using one of these sites as your single center for communicating with clients is a good idea, looks highly professional, and gives you added features and benefits to your workflow that you don't get by using email alone.

---

[32] www.zoho.com
[33] www.freshbooks.com
[34] www.hiveage.com

That said, I don't use them, except with clients who insist on it, because my workflow is already set up differently. For me, it's not worth the time it would take to reorganize the way I already do everything. If I was starting from scratch, as you may be, I'd definitely use one of these applications/sites as my portal for all client-related activities.

If you have many smaller client jobs going on with your freelance writing, rather than one or two large novel projects, I might recommend another option—using Trello[35] for project management. If you use Google Drive and Paypal, as I do, then Trello does everything you need to manage multiple clients and projects.

Content Mills/Work Sites

There are several content mills that are worth joining, especially as you work toward getting your first few paying gigs. After you set up your profiles, search for writing gigs that match your abilities and desires (such as genres).

In the beginning, take anything that comes along regardless of pay rate, to improve site ratings and build portfolio. Quality clients won't hire contractors who

---

[35] www.trello.com

have no track record on that site, so focus on finding the kind of work that you want to do in the long run— but don't turn other gigs away.

Once you have a contract, send the client a note to reassure them you can meet the deadline, look forward to working with them, and will contact them directly if you have any questions about the work.

In order of importance, the top 3 "content mills" are—

Upwork - formerly oDesk and elance

Upwork[36] is the largest, busiest of all the freelance content mills. You can find some excellent clients here if you sift through the bad ones. If you are just learning to write novels and have not yet written your own, Upwork is fantastic for the sheer volume of work suitable for beginners.

Why would you want a lower-paying gig? There are several reasons to aim low when you're just starting out.

1. There are so many of these ghostwriting projects that you're assured of getting someone to take a chance on you.

---

[36] www.upwork.com

2. Yes, you'll earn less at first but, on the other hand, they don't expect perfection. You won't damage your reputation with clients as you improve your skills, learning to write using this low-hanging fruit.

3. Most of them are for short books. If you can write 2,500 words per day, five days per week, that's 12,500 words per week. You won't make much money per hour at that speed, true, but no one does when they first start out. You have to get references and testimonials, and by writing 1-4 short books per month, you'll build that up quickly!

4. The more practice you get, the faster you'll become. I bang out about 1,000 words per hour, up from 750 words when I first started ghostwriting fiction. That's without trying too hard, and getting up every twenty minutes, making coffee, etc. Imagine if you treated it like a full-time job with regular job-style breaks? That's a minimum of 6,000 words per day, and even with a low per-word rate, you'd make up for some of that in volume. You'll have no problem whatsoever making fast-food wages right out of the gate, and it only goes up from there.

5. The more books you've written, the more client references and testimonials you'll have. It's easy to go from starting rates (probably equivalent to minimum wage) to professional rates, the bottom tier of which is about $20 an hour when everything is factored in. It goes up from there, too.

Upwork is *overloaded* with people hiring ghostwriters at cheap rates to write romance novellas. I've never written a romance novel, so I had to dig a bit deeper to find my preferred genres, but not by much more. If you're willing to ghostwrite romances, you'll *never be out of clients.*

The drawback to Upwork is that they take a high percentage of your income when you first begin working with a particular client. It's in your best interest to find someone who will want multiple books from you on an ongoing basis, because as you do more work with one client, Upwork takes less and less for their fees.

PeoplePerHour

PeoplePerHour[37] is great for ghostwriting shorter content like blog posts, but you can also find novels

---

[37] www.peopleperhour.com

and novellas here. There aren't as many gigs as on Upwork, but PPH takes less of your money in fees (15% vs Upwork's 20%). The fees don't go down as you do more work with each client, as they do with Upwork, but they aren't as high to begin with. PPH's fee comes out when you transfer the money to your own accounts, not when the client pays you.

Note: PPH recently set a minimum withdrawal fee of $3.50. Don't withdraw funds until you've accumulated $25 or more because if you withdraw with less than the minimum fee will effectively be much greater than 15%.

Indeed

Indeed[38] is a great general site for freelance writing gigs. You can find a lot of shorter projects here for freelance writing, on top of novels.

There are many sites out there for freelance writers, but these are the three I recommend to begin with. Create a profile for each. Try to keep the content and images/branding the same as your LinkedIn profile. Again, you want to keep your "personal brand" the same across all your platforms.

---

[38] www.indeed.com

Job Considerations

As a ghostwriter, it's vital to have a good work process. It makes your life easier, but also makes your clients' lives easier. It marks you as a professional, which you most definitely are. And most importantly, having a single process will greatly reduce mistakes and miscommunications while speeding up the process.

First, you have to decide if there are topics and genres you won't write. For example, many ghostwriters aren't comfortable writing erotica or stories with children being harmed, so they won't take such gigs. Set your limits *before* searching so you aren't tempted to take a juicy gig that demands you write material you aren't comfortable with. If you don't like the story, neither will the client and their readers.

So where do you start?

I recommend every new ghostwriter first submit proposals for short romance novels at Upwork and

PeoplePerHour. romance is the best way to get started, simply because that genre has the most clients looking for writers. About half of all books sold are romances. An example of a proposal is included in the SAMPLES appendix.

What if you don't like romance?

There's no reason you can't start by looking for science fiction or fantasy book gigs, but it will take longer to find them. Also, because there are fewer such clients, a mistake will affect you more and for longer. Keep that in mind before you dismiss romance novellas and novels as your gateway to ghostwriting.

Then comes the paperwork

Once you agree to a price, it's time for the contract. The content mills all allow you to include specific terms in your contracts, handled through the site itself.

You'll also have to sign and return an NDA (non-disclosure agreement). You can either print, sign, and fax/scan the NDA and contract, or you can just use a site that lets you digitally sign documents. I use

PDFEscape[39] for this, but there are other sites, and even Google Chrome addons.

Digital is faster, more secure, and frankly, more environmentally friendly.

---

[39] www.pdfescape.com

On Contracts

Contracts are documents that legally bind both parties to do or not to do certain things. Those things are spelled out in *clauses*. However, an official contract isn't the only option. There's also something known as a "letter of understanding," which is just as enforceable in court but offers a bit more leeway and a bit more tolerance for the occasional misstatement.

Whether you use a contract or a letter of understanding, though, you'll have to negotiate these clauses to arrive at an agreement that meets your needs and also the client's.

Clauses

There are a few key contract clauses that should be included in every contract you sign so that everything is spelled out from the scope of work to the projected billings.

- **Length of work** - the total number of words for which they will pay.

- **Cost per word** - this can be as low as ½-cent per word when you're just starting out, but goes up as you gain experience, references, and testimonials. Try to get at least 1c/word when starting out, but I wouldn't walk away from a lower rate until you have experience ghostwriting.

- **Deadlines** - Often just a final deadline, but sometimes a deadline for each 10k words or other breakdown of the total word count. If the project will be broken into sub-parts, these are called Milestones, and you get paid at each milestone as I'll discuss under the billing process, a bit later.

- **Payout** - Will you be paid for each milestone? Half up front and half at the end? All of it at the end? Starting out, I recommend accepting payment on completion if the client wants that.

  - If you're working under Upwork or PeoplePerHour, even though you may be taking payment on completion, demand they put half the total payout into escrow.

- If you're working on milestones, demand that the next milestone payment is in escrow before you'll begin writing.

- This protects you from fraud, which is common if you ignore my advice.

- **Conference Calls** - Some clients want daily or weekly conference calls. I have no problem with this, but my time is valuable. I insist on an hourly rate for such calls, payable as we go (weekly, usually). Put this in your terms! I don't charge for email communications, however, and neither should you—this encourages clients to use email to talk to you, which is to your benefit (and sanity).

- **Ownership** - be sure your contract states that you have no ownership of the work, and that this is "work for hire." This protects you from litigation if the book doesn't sell well, or if the client adds plagiarized content without your knowledge.

- **Royalties** - I would never accept a contract that pays me in royalties. I get paid when I do the work, not when the client makes money—if they ever do. Half the novels I've written never got published, and if I worked on royalties, I wouldn't have been paid at all for hundreds of hours of work.

- **Do not agree to sign a non-compete agreement!** That will prevent you from taking other gigs in the same genre, and it isn't reasonable for them to ask, but they sometimes will. Refuse such a requirement and, if necessary, walk away from the gig and find another.

Letter of Understanding

The LOU, or Letter of Understanding, is a legally-binding document that is written in everyday layman's terms instead of legalese. I strongly prefer these to traditional contracts, partly because they are easier to understand.

Another benefit, however, is that while a contract is judged in court based on the letter of the contract only, a letter of understanding is judged on the *intent* of the clauses. There's wiggle room for both you and the client to enforce what you meant to say, not what you actually said.

Yes, a contract is more iron-clad than a LOU, but frankly, that fact will almost always "protect" *you*, not the other way around. Service contracts tend to have been originally written by lawyers. Those lawyers almost always were working for a client, not a writer, when they originally drafted the contracts. This means that even example contracts you might find online will generally not be ones you'd want to use.

I've seen some really hairbrained contracts in my time, especially when non-lawyer writers like me try to make our own contracts or try to copy someone else's contract. Often, what you think a contract says isn't quite what the lawyers and judges will think it says.

A good LOU will cover all the same terms a contract will, but the LOU states each clause plainly, in everyday English. I include an example of a Letter of Understanding in the SAMPLES chapter of this book.

Negotiating Terms

Although most contracts contain the same types of clauses, the details can vary tremendously. The ones you can normally expect to see in a ghostwriting contract—and you should add them, if they aren't included—are pretty straightforward:

- You agree to write a certain number of words at an agreed-upon rate per word

- You agree to finish it by a specific deadline

- For your writing, you will be paid either at the start of each milestone, half up front and half on completion, or some other simple arrangement

- You acknowledge that the writing will be done as work-for-hire, giving you no rights to the work, its copyright, and its sales or royalties

- You agree never to tell anyone that you wrote it. If you're the co-author, you agree not to say that you did the lion's share of the writing, much less all of it.

Overcoming Obstacles

But what if they don't want to pay the rate you want, or want to pay upon acceptance of the finished work? What if they offer an impossible deadline? These things happen a lot because the client is often not a writer, themselves.

If the rate of pay is too low, about all you can do is read books on the art of negotiating. I've found that if you have experience and references you can refer to, you can sometimes get the client to realize it's worth a bit more for a better finished manuscript and that you're a professional who knows how to work with clients, making the process less of a headache for them.

If you don't yet have experience and references, your only option will usually be to accept it with a smile or walk away from the deal. Expect to be paid less (sometimes a lot less) for your first couple of projects, though. It's worth it to get happy customers as references.

If they want to pay you at the end only, on the other hand, it's pretty easy to pitch the milestones arrangement. Although it protects you from getting scammed, from your client's perspective it lets them back out if they don't like your writing style, without having to pay the entire contract price. Once you tell them that, they almost always like the idea of paying on milestones.

With deadline issues, I explain that I know how fast I write and how long it takes me to self-edit. I tell them what I need, based on my experience. They either accept a later date or I walk away, because I will never accept a contract I'm not 100% sure I can finish by the deadline, risking my credibility and reputation. *Always meet your deadlines.*

Estimating Your Writing Time

If you don't yet have the experience to know how long it takes you to write *X pages* on *topic Y,* or fiction in *X genre*, then what do you do? Well, you can point to the website I gave that lists the market-standard writing and editing rates.

It says that the average per-hour writing pace is "1-3 ms pgs/hr." That's one to three manuscript pages per hour. As you'll recall, I said that the standard is always 250 words per page.

The average writer, according to that page, can draft 500 words per hour. Those same guidelines say you'll need about the same amount of time for your revisions (i.e., heavy editing). The client should be happy to receive an edited draft; a professional would never give a rough draft to the client.

Here's something you may not have considered, though: You will likely need about 20% of the writing time for formatting and client communications.

What if research is needed? It often is, even if you wouldn't think so at first glance.

- If the book is modern-era fiction, you'll need about 1 hour of research for every 10,000 words in the story, mostly spent researching locations and city guides.

- If it's a period-based story, triple that to 3 hours per 10,000 words!

- If it's off-Earth sci fi, you may not need any research time, and the same goes for fantasy.

- If it's nonfiction, I can't give specific guidelines on how long research will take you. That will vary based on your previous knowledge of the subject. Regardless, you must balance the hours you claim versus the client's budget needs or they'll find another writer. You won't usually spend more time researching than writing, however, so if you're at a total loss, you may consider adding research time equal to the time you allotted for writing.

- *Always add 10% to the time you* think *it will* *take you.*

Example Time Estimation

You have approval to write a 50,000-word novel for your client. Let's say the book is to be an urban paranormal romance story. According to this system, you will need:

- 100 hours to write the story (50,000/500)

- 100 hours to edit your draft (50,000/500)

- 20 hours for communicating with your client (20% of writing time)

- 5 hours of research (1 hour per 10,000 words)

- 22.5 hours for a built-in safety margin (subtotal + 10%)

Your total example gig's required time is now 247.5 hours. Round up to 250 working hours to complete the project.

Figuring Out Your Deadline

Never assume you'll be able to write for the length of time each day that you think you will. If you believe you can write for a solid six hours per day, plan for five. Things come up, and you'd be surprised how much time is spent going to the bathroom or getting another cup of coffee.

Divide the number of hours you'll need by your conservative estimate of how many hours per day you want to work. Our example was five hours per day, so we'll go with that. You'd want to give yourself [250 / 5 = 50] work days. Working five days per week to get up to 50 work days, you can see that the ghostwriter should ask for 10 weeks before the deadline hits.

You'll probably finish well before the deadline. Why? You'll write faster than you allowed for in your estimate, your research won't take as long as you thought, you'll find yourself working for eight hours instead of five, on some days, and you sometimes won't be able to resist writing on a Saturday.

With this buffer, however, if you had to make an emergency trip to Seattle to visit your sister-in-law in the hospital, you can recover. You can still meet the deadline. Remember, a professional always meets their deadline.

If the client isn't willing to adjust the deadline date, you must consider whether you're willing to work longer hours or more days each week in order to meet it. If you aren't willing to do those things, then you're be better off politely declining and finding another gig.

The Revisions Clause

It's also important to include a statement in your contract or LOU that explains that any revisions required are outside the scope of this deadline: "*If the client wishes the writer to revise submitted materials within the terms of this [contract or letter of understanding], the client understands that such revisions may occur outside the listed deadline for draft completion.*"

Having said that, I usually work on revisions while I'm writing subsequent chapters. I simply work a bit longer each day. This way the client feels well taken care of, because I've exceeded the contract terms. Outstanding customer service is vital for getting references and testimonials. Which leads us to…

Portfolio Clause

Long-time ghostwriter Gretchen Anthony introduced me to this idea in a fantastic post on TheWriteLife.com[40]. She includes a clause in her contracts that asks to use the work in her portfolio as a writing example. As she explains, "*It states that I reserve the right to include the contracted work in part or in full within my professional portfolio.*"

She goes on to say that for books (rather than blog posts, etc.), she asks to use an excerpt. She then negotiates with the client to find a word count limit such as 500 words (i.e. two pages).

I think it's worth trying. At worst, they say no. I think I'd state in the contract that I agree to include it in my portfolio in private communications with prospective clients rather than on my website, just to make them feel more comfortable with the idea.

---

[40] TheWriteLife - https://thewritelife.com/build-a-writing-portfolio/

Along the same lines, this gives me the idea of adding a "Testimonial" clause, in which the client agrees to provide me with a 1-line *and* a 1-paragraph testimonial after the project is finished, which I can use on different social media platforms and my website. If I don't like their testimonial, I obviously wouldn't use it.

Negotiating Online or by Phone

A lot of times, you'll talk to a client not only through email but also Messenger, Skype, on the phone, etc. Anything you agree to within those applications is just as binding as the terms you discuss by email—even the things you don't remember talking about.

You could pore through miles of chat logs to find every detail you talked about, and struggle to revise the contract to match, but you're assured of missing something eventually. The better, simpler solution is to add a clause to your contract that limits the entire agreement to only what is written in the contract up until date the contract is signed. Anything you agree to after that is still binding, but hopefully you worked out all the details *before* signing contracts…

If you use a letter of understanding rather than a contract, as I recommend, simply add something in normal English, for example, "*This letter of understanding constitutes the entirety of the agreement. Any items discussed or agreed to prior to this letter, but which are not included in this letter, are not binding on either party."*

Do try to make sure you include in your contract anything you and the client agreed to beforehand. Especially if it benefits or protects you, they should be added to the contract and not just left to memory.

Workflow

Once the contract is signed and agreed to and money has been put in escrow (if using a wordmill), or once your first milestone is paid up (if you found the client elsewhere), it's time to get to work.

Outline Approval

I've discussed outlining above, and I won't go into details on that here except to say that you're costing yourself money and headaches if you don't use outlines. For more on *fast, easy outlining*, then see my short ebook, *3 Easy Outlines for Ghostwriters*[41].

It's important to have client approval of the outline before you begin drafting the story because once the client has "buy in" on the outline and characters, they

---

[41] 3 Easy Outlines for Ghostwriters - http://smarturl.it/GWritingResources

are much less likely to have issues with something later.

Also, let them know that the outline may change slightly as ideas come up while you're writing. Even so, it shouldn't change in any major way without stopping to get client approval of the changes, which slows you down and costs you money. Minor changes are okay, and unavoidable, but if you come up with a fantastic idea that requires you to revise the last half of the outline, don't. Write the book the client agreed to and keep your cool idea for your writing swipe file.

If you use Hiveword for outlining and story bible creation[42], as I strongly suggest, the app will print out your entire story, characters and all, as a PDF file you can send the client. Sending a professionally assembled story bible *for no extra effort* is a fantastic way to make that client remember you (in a good way).

I like to post my story bible where the client can get to it, such as Google Drive (rather than by email), and say, "*work begins in [24 or 48] hours unless you wish to see revisions. The time required to make such revisions to the outline will be appended to all*

---

[42] Hiveword for Outlining & Story Bible - http://smarturl.it/GWritingResources

*contracted deadlines, so that we can be on the same
page when work begins."*

That strategy motivates the client to accept your
outline as-is or with minor changes, and if they take a
week to approve it, that time is added to the deadline
instead of making you work frantically to catch up. It's
win-win.

The Writing Process

Because I use Google Docs and Google Drive
whenever possible, my process is pretty simple.

1. Create a folder for each new project.

2. In that folder, create a subfolder called Archives.
    Old versions of anything go in there for
    accountability purposes, and only your most
    recent version is visible in the main folder. Trust
    me—I have accidentally worked on an older
    version, and it's a frustrating time-waster.

3. I create a new document for *each chapter* shown
    in my outline. If I'm writing a book without
    chapters, then I'll divide it into equal chunks of
    5,000 to 10,000 words each. For example, I'd
    make five doc files for a 50,000-word book.

4. I name these files "TITLEWORD-ChX-v1," using a word from the title and the chapter number (or -PtX- if divided into chunks). The X is for the chapter or part number, obviously, and "v1" stands for Version 1. **Example:** *HOLLOW-Ch4-v1*

5. When I finish drafting one chapter, I immediately move on to drafting the next.

6. When I'm halfway through the next one, or when the next one is finished (depending on length), I make a copy of the previous document, name it "v2," and thoroughly self-edit the v2 file. The v1 file gets moved to the Archive subfolder.

7. Once I've finished editing v2 as well as I can, I send it to the client as a Word document for approval, changes, or comments.

8. If they want changes, I'll save a new v3 document just as I did for v2, implement the changes, and send v3 back. I'll go back and forth on a chapter until the client is satisfied, or I decide they've reached their revisions limit as stated in the contract.

The reason I wait awhile before editing my drafts is to give myself distance. I can't stress enough how important this is in terms of the quality of your final copy.

Overall, this process is simple, efficient, and avoids "version control errors," where the client is revising one version and you're working on another. It's stressful to have to merge the two, and if it's your fault (which it always seems to be, even if it's not), then you won't be able to bill for the time it takes to integrate the two versions.

Billing Process

Your contract states when you'll get paid. Sometimes the plan is half up front and half on completion, or all up front, but I push hard for milestones if it's over 10k words. I prefer one milestone per 10k words. I'll go as high as one per 25k words for clients I've worked well with in the past, and whom I trust. See the chapter on CONTRACTS for more on this.

PayPal Invoicing

If you use PayPal for invoicing—which I recommend, unless the project is through a content mill—then send the client an invoice at the beginning of work for the

TOTAL amount you expect to be paid for the gig. Click the checkbox that says "*Allow partial payment.*"

Another box then pops up asking for the minimum payment allowed. If you're billing half up front and half on completion, then this minimum amount is 50% of the contract value. If you are on milestones, divide the total by the number of milestones. With 5 milestones, divide the total by 5.

By doing this, you only have to manage one invoice per gig, and you can easily see how much of it has been paid already. Always get paid for the last installment before giving them the next batch of writing!

The reason I prefer milestones to payment on completion is that it protects *both the client and you*, making it an easy sell. The client doesn't have to trust you'll finish the book after they already paid you half of it, and you don't have to trust that they'll pay you at the end, because payment occurs as you go. The most either of you could be swindled for is one installment.

Content Mill Invoicing

If you're using Upwork or other content mill, the process is different. You have to use their billing process from within the site, but the process isn't much different. At each milepost, you ask them to release the money already in escrow to you, and put money into escrow for the next milestone.

Once you've been paid, *the money goes into your account on that site*. Connect your content mill accounts to your PayPal or bank account so you can withdraw those funds!

I'll repeat what I said earlier—your life will be much simpler if you use PayPal and get a PayPal debit card.

- Receive all income to PayPal, and use PayPal to make all your business-related purchases and bill payments.

- If you wish to use money for yourself, then *transfer the money from PayPal to your bank account first*, and then buy the item from your regular bank account instead of your PayPal.

  - This is called a *draw* and is how you take business profits for yourself, since you aren't on salary or wages as a sole proprietor.

  - This way, you easily mark money coming into your bank account as being something you don't need to pay taxes on—you'll already pay taxes on it for your business.

- ○ Talk to an accountant if you are set up with a different form of ownership than simple Sole Proprietor, such as an S-corporation.

- If you need to add personal money to PayPal to pay a business expense (your internet or cell phone, for example), it's a *loan* from you to your business. As a Liability, you get to pay yourself back later without that money being taxed twice.

This is the simplest, easiest way to guarantee your business and personal funds don't get mixed up, and to clearly mark what is business income and what isn't.

If you ever get audited, this will be *vital* to getting through clear and unscathed. You can get audited for activity from *years ago*, so this ensures electronic records remain of every business expense and income, all in one place, separated from personal records so it's crystal clear which money is which.

If I could only recommend one thing to do as a ghostwriter, other than getting clients, *this would be it*. It's that important.

What Should I Get Paid?

You can find average hourly rates at the Editorial Freelancers Association[43] website. These are pretty accurate for well-established writers and editors (not including, ironically, ghostwriters like you), but they list these as an hourly rate or price per page.

NOTE: A "page" is always 250 words for billing purposes!

Fiction ghostwriters make a lot less than what the site shows—those rates are for writers doing memoirs and autobiographies for celebrities or CEOs. Established fiction ghostwriters make 2-6 cents per word, unless you land a ghostwriting gig with a famous author like Patterson. On the bright side, fiction ghostwriters will never want for more work after becoming an established, credible freelancer.

As a new ghostwriter, you'll pretty much take what you can get, but you want to work toward higher rates. If you have long-term clients, ask for another penny-per-word after you've worked with them for a year, or an extra half-cent per word after six months.

---

[43] Editorial Freelancers Association - www.the-efa.org/res/rates.php

Most ghostwriting clients want a per-word rate, with a lower and upper word limit set in the contracts before you begin writing. Some, however, will want an hourly rate. In these cases, you must convert the per-word rate to an hourly one.

The average writer will write two pages per hour including time spent on the outline, communicating with the client, and so on. Each page is *always* 250 words for this purpose, so the average writer produces 500 words per hour (WPH). At 2 cents per word, that's $10/hour—but don't worry, your actual writing speed will quickly improve if it hasn't already, increasing your effective hourly rate.

Let's show an example of this in action. If you are contracted to write a novel of 50,000 words, that's (supposedly) going to take you 100 hours. You could expect to earn $1,000 for the book, or $10/hour.

If I made only $0.02 per word and write at 1,000 WPH, I would make $20/hour. *Speed is life.* That's why outlining is so darn important.

How realistic is 1,000 WPH? Well, there's 60 minutes in an hour and the average person puts out about 35 words per minute (WPM). Your WPM will go up the more you write, but this average person will write 35

WPM x 60 minutes/hour = 2,100 WPH. At 70 WPM, I can potentially write 4,200 WPH.

That rate doesn't include coffee breaks, outlining, answering the phone, interacting with spouse and kids, or thinking about what to write. Still, I think you can see that with a reasonable amount of effort, $20/hour is pretty easy to accomplish at 2 cents per word.

Talking to Clients About Budget

For the most part, discussing the budget with clients is easy. They'll tell you what they want to pay you, and you say yes or no. Use the rates website I listed above for high-end ghostwriting, or the rates I provide you in this book for genre fiction.

If you're writing a biography, or if you are writing a nonfiction book that requires you to interview subject matter experts, you'll definitely need to pitch an hourly rate for interviewing and research. I suggest starting at $20 per hour, earlier in your career, rising to $40 per hour if you specialize in only a few topics.

The reason you need to charge per hour for this is that you don't know how much time you'll spend in research and interviews, and you need to be paid for that time. In your proposal, separate the writing rate (usually per word) from research/interviews (always per hour).

Later, when you have lots of experience, you'll be able to guesstimate how many hours research will take, and can convert that into a per-word rate that works for you. Until then, however, you'll only shortchange yourself if you agree only to a per-word rate unless it's very high.

Most of your ghostwriting will be fiction, so you won't need to deal with hourly rates because per-word is the way to go for that. Fiction clients usually don't like hourly rates, because who knows how many hours a writer will claim? It's impossible for a client to set a budget when using an hourly rate with a new author they haven't worked with before.

Q&A: Other Work Questions

Here are a few questions that I get asked fairly regularly, and my responses. These are based on my own experiences, so you may find different answers for some of these.

Q: What should I do if the client offers to credit me as co-author?

That depends. If I want my name associated with the book's content *and* genre, *and* I think the quality is good enough that I want my name on it ten years from now, I'd accept. You won't likely be offered royalties, but it's worth it for the credit.

The second option, if the answer to any of the above is *no*, is to decline. You have two choices as to how you do so. Either politely decline by saying that you don't want your name in public (or some other polite excuse), or ask them to use your "pen name," which lets you write more in that genre later with a bit of a head start.

Most of the time, especially if you haven't written at least 3-4 novels already, you're going to want to use the second option.

Q: If the contract is for 80k words but I write 87k, what do I do?

Especially in the beginning of your career, *even with outlining*, you'll find this happens a lot. If you don't use an outline, you will go over your word count every time, and by many more words. **Use an outline!** The time you spend writing extra words is time you probably aren't going to get paid for, so minimize how often it happens and limit the number of words by which you go over your target. Outlining is just something you'll need to get used to if you want to succeed. Okay, enough with the Public Service Announcement. To answer your question...

I submit the extra words anyway, without expecting to get paid for them.

- The client doesn't have to pay for them because they aren't part of the contract

- You can't demand the client pay you more

- You can't withhold the story from them until they do pay more

- The time it would take to cut the word count down would be unpaid!

What I do instead is to tell the client something like:

Dear Clientperson,

*[This is where your normal discussion about completing the book goes. Then, below this, you **add** something like the following...]*

One more thing. The novel went about 7k words over. I think the story is told the way it needs to be told, so rather than cut them out, I'm just sending them. Enjoy! I hope it's not an inconvenience. On our next novel, I'll try to make sure I end up closer to the contract word count.

Sincerely,

Yourname Goeshere

About half the time, the client will end up paying you for them anyway because they get really thrilled when you deliver more than they paid for. Under-promise, over-deliver! The client doesn't have to know it was an accident, and you definitely don't need to inform them that you sent more words because it was a better use of your time than cutting the novel down to the contracted word count.

In other words, even though it's your mistake, you make them feel like it's just a free gift from you to them because you care so much about the story.

Even if they don't pay you for those words—and you should never even mention the idea!—they'll remember you for it. If they like your writing style and so on, they'll come back to you before going to someone else. That's how you get repeat clients. In fact, I habitually go about 2%-5% over what I contracted for, so my clients always get a great deal—and almost always hire me for future projects.

Q: Can I still use the milestone payments system if I don't want to share the content with the client until the book is completed?

Absolutely. The only different step would be that you don't submit the chapters as you edit them, but instead send them all together when you're done writing the whole book. If you wish to do that, remember to modify your Letter of Understanding (presented in the APPENDIX).

You could still use the self-editing system I describe in this book, however, going over each chapter when you're done drafting the chapter after it. Or you can simply do all the self-editing after you complete the novel drafting process. The process to determine the deadline you need to ask for, included in this book, accounts for editing time. If you meet your daily writing goals, you will have enough time to edit at the end or as you go, whichever you prefer.

The reason I like to self-edit and submit my chapters as I go, rather than at the end, is mainly because clients love it. They feel more involved because they *are* more involved. Better yet, it lets them see and feel your progress, providing all the reassurance they need that you are doing the job on time. Also, they often have great ideas that you can incorporate, or use later. And the best reason of all: It makes the client feel like you're their partner instead of a service provider under contract.

And *that* is where completion bonuses, repeat clients, and word-of-mouth referrals are born.

Q: How much input will the client have?

Usually, not a lot after writing begins. They may want to see a few changes or corrections after they review finished work, but otherwise they will leave you alone. This is especially true if you got them to buy into your outline—another vital reason to get them to approve an outline rather than "pantsing" the novel.

Sometimes, however, the client will provide you with an outline they've created. In these cases, they tend to have a clear idea in mind, and know how they want it to look. Because you can't read their minds, if the outline isn't clear enough, you'll end up making a lot of revisions. If they provide an outline, you definitely want to take their outline and get all the clarifications you need before writing. In these cases, I also like to improve on their outline by adding scene summaries or other revisions and sending it back to them as the "working structure document." Getting that approved will save tons of time later in the process, and remember, *time is money.* Literally.

By calling it a working structure document instead of an outline, you avoid getting their ego involved and they hopefully don't become upset or insulted that you "didn't like" their masterful outline. That's not the message you want to convey!

The message you want to send is that you are a professional writer, and you don't get upset over revisions. And you shouldn't, because "it ain't personal." Your client probably isn't a professional freelance writer and for them it can be very personal. Simply by calling your revised outline something different, you can avoid most of that drama.

Some clients will want to talk on the phone or through Skype to regularly discuss your writing progress. Say no! Unless they want to pay you for your time, it isn't fair of them to expect you to spend professional time talking to them for free.

There's a solution, though.

I usually tell them at the very beginning that they can have two 15 minute calls throughout the course of the book *at no cost,* plus one free 30-minute call before beginning, if needed. It's worth an hour of my time to provide excellent customer service. Anything more than this, however, means they need to pay me. I'm fine with $10/hour to talk to them, instead of my usual hourly rate.

Other ghostwriters bill for even that time, or offer it for free but actually add it to their proposed price. How you handle this is up to you. You may decide you need $20/hour, or even some other rate. Just be sure you're crystal clear in your CONTRACT TERMS about the amount you charge for the extra time spent in client communications.

Once in awhile, you'll get a client who wants constant, repeated revisions, eating your time even after writing is done. My very first fiction ghostwriting client had me make *six or seven complete revisions*. I spent more time talking to him and revising the work than I did drafting the novel! I hadn't put terms in our contract for the time that took, and I wanted to make my first client happy to get a reference, so I just had to eat that time. A hard lesson…

Learn from my mistakes. Put an hourly rate on conference calls and limit your revisions to *one* revision, totaling no more than 25% of each individual chapter or segment (not 25% of the book as a whole).

Additional revision work should be paid at a per-hour rate that is higher than your conference calls rate. I add $5/hour. Because I charge only $10/hour for conference calls, additional revisioning is done at a rate of $15/hour. It's not a money-maker for me, but the goal is to limit the client's demands on my time by setting expectations and being clear that your time costs them money. When your time equals their dollars, they stop being unreasonably demanding.

Yep, put those clauses in your contracts. Trust me, you'll be glad you did.

Q: What if a client is unsatisfied with the book you write?

If you're working on milestones, as I suggest you do every time and always, then they can walk away after paying you for the one or two installments you already delivered. Neither of you is out much time or money.

If you ignored my advice and contracted for half up front, half at the end, then you may need to knuckle down and do extra work to make them happy, just to get that last half of your payment. It's usually worth an extra ten hours in revisions to get the other half paid and to create a happy customer. After this happens to you once, you'll understand why I only work on milestones or up-front, unless I know that client very, very well.

Every once in a great while, you'll get a client who will never be happy, no matter what you do for them. If you've already spent an extra ten hours on the project to make them happy, unpaid, and they're just as unhappy as they were to begin with, politely explain that you have other contracts and can't work on this project any further. You allotted the time you knew it would take, in your contract, and now you have other signed contracts to fulfill. Even if you don't have another contract, it makes a good excuse and you can use the saved time to find another one.

Because they're unhappy with the work, consider agreeing to only take a half payment on the remainder. If you're lucky, they'll pay it and you'll have been paid 3/4 of the contracted amount. If you're unlucky, walk away and thank them for their time. You're just out of luck for the rest of the money they owe you, unless you're willing and able to take the client to court.

Note: If you do decide to take them to court, never announce it. Let your attorney announce to the client that they are being sued.

Q: What do you do if a client refuses to pay? Do you own the writing?

If the client refuses to make a payment, there is little you can do. If you followed my advice to work and bill on milestones, then you are only out the time and money for one or two chapters.

Technically, any work they don't pay you for is owned by you. You maintain copyright on the words used in the unpaid portion until the terms of the contract are met, meaning payment.

If you're only out one or two chapters, the best thing to do is let them have what you've already sent, stop writing, and thank them for their time. Ask for a positive testimonial.

On the other hand, if you ignore my advice and you wrote a whole book for payment at the end or half at the end, you have to make a decision as to whether you want to let them use it and whether you want to use it yourself.

Either way, I'd let them know you still own the copyright to the unpaid portion of the book, and they are not legally allowed to use it until they pay you for it. I would offer to take a lesser payment, saying I understand sometimes people's circumstances change, because I'd rather be paid something than nothing.

If you decide to rewrite any portion they paid for and then publish the book yourself, you can expect to hear from a lawyer. You'd likely win in court, but is it worth it? Lawyer fees could far outweigh any income from publishing the book yourself.

My advice would be to just let it go. Send the letter I mentioned (by email is fine) and move on, putting the whole mess into an archive. I might check Copyscape every 3-6 months to see if they'd published it anyway. If they have, then let Amazon know that you own the copyright so it gets taken down. Check the Amazon rankings, and if it's a bestseller, only then consider lawyers. If it's not, forget lawyers and be happy that Amazon took it down and marked them as a plagiarist. Possibly, put the word out on social media. That works both ways, though—they'll certainly already have slandered you before they ever publish it. It may still be best to just let it go, because everyone loses in a so-called Facebook War, guaranteed.

Q: Do you always have to sign an NDA and Non-Compete Agreement?

No. You should *never* sign a non-compete, because it limits what else you can write to earn a living. However, you'll almost always have to sign an NDA (non-disclosure agreement) that prevents you from telling anyone you wrote it. You can't even tell your spouse, legally. If you do let the cat out of the bag, you'll get sued for whatever damages the client thinks you might have cost them, and you'll probably lose in court. An NDA is normal—sign it, obey it. The non-compete agreement is unreasonable, and I'd walk away from any client who insisted on one.

Q: Do you ever get credit for your writing?

As a ghostwriter, you will rarely get public credit for your writing. Only if your contract states that you'll be listed as co-author, or if they tell you an NDA isn't needed, can you claim credit to it. Yet even if you're the co-author, you still can't disclose that you wrote the whole thing.

Also, the co-author spot is rarely offered or given to ghostwriters in fiction writing. It's more common in celebrity bios and nonfiction books, but even there you may not get to talk about it. You can ask if he or she will let you be listed as co-author, but I wouldn't insist if it will mean losing the deal.

Consider this, however: even if you can get the co-author listing, *do you really want to?* Maybe... But since you have no control over the book's final form, and you don't know if the client will hire a professional editor (much less whether that editor is any good), consider declining having your name listed as co-author even if the client offers. Or you might request they use a pen name for you, rather than your real name.

Many people have a hard time accepting that they don't get credit for their writing, as a ghostwriter (see the previous section, "Letting Go of the Nut"), but to be a *professional* means coming to grips with that fact. Deal with your personal and emotional issues with the idea before you dive into ghostwriting.

Instead of getting credit, what you can do is to ask the client if he or she will be a reference for you to your future prospective clients. Maybe they'll give you a testimonial to put on your web page (possibly under a pen name). Often, happy clients will give you a great quote for your testimonials page, but also insist on using another name, or even initials. That's fine!

Q: How do you build your portfolio if you can't reference your work?

This is a tough question to answer. First, look for co-authoring opportunities, for which you get credit along with the main listed author (even though you wrote it all).

Second, consider a PORTFOLIO CLAUSE in your contracts. I do not make this clause a requirement, but I do ask.

Third, I give a few tips in the GETTING CLIENTS section of this book that might help.

Beyond that, please understand that your prospective clients already know you can't reveal what you've worked on previously. They won't be bothered when you tell them those works are under NDA, and they will instead happily check your testimonials and references. That's why it is so important to get legitimate testimonials for your site and references you can give them privately.

Because your clients don't want you to reveal your participation in their books, they'll respect you for keeping your prior work secret to honor your NDA, and your use of volunteer references. Not all your prospects will read your testimonials or contact references, but most do. Keep adding those items to your lists whenever you can. They'll take those references seriously in lieu of a portfolio.

Getting Clients

Finding new clients is the perennial problem for new ghostwriters. Rarely, you might luck into a long-term relationship with a client who just hires writers and then markets the heck out of the books. These people are basically professional marketers, not writers, and you could get a lot of ongoing work from them. They tend to be more concerned with speed than quality, but that's not always true.

Note: some long-term clients might be willing to let you list them as a co-author of your own books, down the road, letting you grab onto their existing reader base. They may want a split in royalties, but it could be worth doing until you have your own back catalog of books built up. As professional marketers, such a person can only help your early books get noticed.

The top 5 basic ways to get clients, in no particular order, are content mills, advertising, word-of-mouth, nonprofits, quid pro quo, and social media. I'll give you a brief consideration of each of these, so that you can use as many channels as possible to try to find new clients.

Content Mills

Content mills such as Upwork are discussed in detail elsewhere under CONTENT MILLS/WORK SITES. You should definitely make use of them, especially early in your ghostwriting career.

Advertising

Paid advertising is iffy, but you might experiment with Facebook promotions to advertise your professional Facebook Page. See if it works, at a cost as low as $10 or $20. If you do try Facebook ads, one option is to use a post that has already scored well compared to your other posts. You already know those are effective in drawing attention.

You may have better luck "advertising" by paying for high search results on job sites and content mills. Some sites will let you pay to have an ad banner placed there

While I have written many email sales letters for clients, I have not tried to manage an email list program of my own for my writing business. There are lots of great books on email marketing, however. If you do experiment with an email newsletter to generate business, please contact me and let me know how it went. I'd love to hear from you!

Social Media and Word of Mouth

Word of mouth and social media are conjoined. If you are active on Facebook groups where some potential clients hang out—including aspiring writers who may have an idea burning a hole in their soul, but may discover they lack the talent to write the novel well—then you can catch the occasional client there simply by being active within the group.

I don't mean hawking your wares, though. No one likes SPAMmers. Instead, I mean by being helpful, answering questions, cheering people's wins, and generally being a good member of the community. This builds trust, and ghostwriting is definitely a trust-based connection with people.

I have been approached to write books several times simply because the prospective client was already familiar with me and my style through Facebook posts and comments. I've even been hired to ghostwrite a single, troublesome chapter in someone else's book!

Social media is worth your time, with two caveats. First, it can drain your productivity completely. You know how much time the book is going to take and how many hours per day, and so on, from the work you did in the FIGURING OUT YOUR DEADLINE segment of this book. During writing hours, turn social media and email *off.* Completely.

Secondly, as a ghostwriter, you must handle your social media activity professionally. Keep personal and business content separate, don't *ever* get involved in a flame war online, and don't spam Groups. People hate spammers. Post, repost, or comment on knowledgeable, helpful articles and they'll find you. Consider setting up separate accounts for personal and work activity, and then *keep them separate.*

On the other hand, after you've ghostwritten your first book and can legitimately claim to be a ghostwriter, it isn't SPAM to post a reply to someone's question that reveals what you do.

For example, it may be appropriate to say, "As a ghostwriter, in my experience, the answer to your question is X, Y, and Z." You aren't promoting your services there, but rather, trying to help someone—and including your credentials to show why you are qualified to present your opinion/solution.

If they are interested in talking about a project, this notifies everyone that you are someone they may wish to talk to. They'll message you directly, then.

Nonprofits

I have ghostwritten two books for nonprofits. They were fun, and I was doing something positive in the world. What I wasn't doing was getting paid! Still, nonprofits will be happy to receive your help in writing a topical book for them, and will often be willing to give you at least co-author credit, if not the byline. They'll almost always be happy to give you a review or testimonial, and to be a professional reference for a future prospective client.

If you're building up your portfolio and resumé, working for nonprofits is a fast and easy way to get experience and client testimony. (And talk to your tax accountant about whether you can claim the hours worked as a deduction on your taxes.)

When pursuing a nonprofit to donate writing time, I recommend you focus on smaller nonprofits that are involved with something you're passionate about. They may not have the resources to have a writer on staff, and you will do your best work for them because you share their passion.

For example, I know a lot about permaculture, sustainable communities, and sustainable agriculture. I mean, *a lot*. I volunteered to write two books for two different permaculture projects in Africa, at no charge and without my byline, just to help them out. You can bet they're happy to be enthusiastic references.

Doing something like this doesn't only give you references, testimonials, and possibly credits. It also builds your experience with writing nonfiction, which is a lucrative market in its own right. Plus, it feels good to use your writing superpowers for the Forces of Good.

Quid Pro Quo

This sneaky trick is neither sneaky nor a trick. It's a perfectly valid method to build up your ghostwriting brand. How do you do it? It's pretty simple, really. You only need to find someone online or in person who knows how to write but is pretty new at it. Preferably someone who is interested in ghostwriting as a career, or at least for an additional stream of income.

Next, you write a novella or novel that they publish under their own name or pen name. After it has been self-published by your partner, you plaster the cover for the book you ghostwrote on your website. You blog about how you "recently ghostwrote *The Sky is Dying* by Mike Smith, and he loved it so much, he let me use it in my portfolio!" On your website, add links to the Amazon page, their client testimony about your service, and list them as a client reference.

Meanwhile, your partner blogs about how they ghostwrote *your* novel, with the cover pictured, and states that you were so satisfied with their work that you allowed them to put "your" book in their portfolio.

In other words, you each ghostwrite a novel for the other person to publish and for you to put in your ghostwriting portfolio.

Not only can this method build experience and portfolio for you both, you might even make some money on sales, especially if you continue to use that pen name down the road for other books in the same genre.

Ideas like these are often called "Guerrilla Marketing," and this was just one example of how people can get creative to legitimately build their portfolio and credentials while gaining experience writing.

Step-by-Step Work Process

Now that you've read the details on each stage of the startup process, where do you actually begin? It's one thing for me to say "... and then you get paid!" and another thing to list the steps involved. That's why I created the following checklist, just for you.

Start at the top, work your way down, and by the time you check off the last item, you'll be a newly minted professional ghostwriter.

Getting Prepared

☒ Get mentally prepared to write for money without your name on the book

☒ Ensure you have a reliable computer and a comfortable, ergonomic desk and chair

☒ Have an available printer, scanner, and headphones with mic

☒ Set up a Gmail address solely for professional use, and connect it to Google Drive

☒ Have Microsoft Office installed, or use Google Documents exclusively until you can get Office

☒ Establish a PayPal account and tie it to your personal bank account. If you have a business bank account for your writing-related business, you can connect that to PayPal instead.

☒ Apply for a PayPal debit card, so you can spend your money without waiting a couple days for it to transfer from PayPal to your bank account, and so you can pay for business expenses from PayPal instead of your personal account

☒ Establish a writing website to show to prospective clients

☒ Set up social media profiles for your writing business. The Profile for each of these should display similar information from your web page's About Me section, and use the same colors/fonts/graphics to establish branding.

- o **Facebook Account or Page** - if you have a personal account, you can simply set up a new Page from it just for your writing

- o **Twitter** - Under URL, put your website or FB Page

- o **Google Plus** (G+) - you will probably only use it for re-posting from your blog or your

Facebook Page, although G+ is every bit as interesting as FB in my opinion

- **Tumblr** - only if you have a blog on your web page

- **LinkedIn** - your virtual resume to validate your claims

  - If you already have a LinkedIn account, add writing-related content to your profile

  - If you don't have one already, set up a new LinkedIn profile and try to make it specific to writing

  - If you don't yet have a writing career to use in creating this profile, then use other things you've done that provide *relevant skills*, or talk about the books you like

- Buffer.com - auto-schedules social media posts to Twitter, Facebook, G+, and other social media platforms

☒ Create a professional-looking email signature at WiseStamp and associate it with your new professional email address

☒ Consider setting up an account with an invoicing/billing service such as Zoho, Freshbooks, or Hiveage, or just use PayPal invoicing

☒ Consider setting up Google Docs templates in Google Drive for various kinds of gigs. I recommend you add them as you go.

At this point, you are ready to begin writing professionally. You have everything you need to do the work and then get paid for it. This list covered the basic things you will definitely need, although there are many other tools, sites, and apps you can use to "work better, smarter, faster."

Finding Clients

☒ Social media activity (especially writing or freelancing-related posts) for a few minutes each day, using Buffer for the best ones. Sometimes mention that you are a ghostwriter.

☒ Check your nearest metropolitan Craigslist for people seeking writers. If you will write blog posts and such also, then add "content creation" to your Craigslist gigs searches.

☒ Create accounts at Upwork, PeoplePerHour, and Indeed

☒ Put up well-written fliers at community bulletin boards such as grocery stores and big-box stores, announcing that you are a ghostwriter who will write for them at a reasonable price

☒ Join Facebook writing groups that focus on beginning writers and book marketing

☒ Create a Twitter List called "Might Need Ghostwriter" or something similar. See TWITTER section, above, for details.

Getting the Contract Signed

☒ On content mills, you must find a relevant job posting and then submit a proposal. Make sure your terms include the items discussed in this book under CONTRACTS, if you wish (some are relevant, some are not).

☒ Outside of content mills, try to use your own contract that covers the items discussed in this book, or submit a revision to their contract removing terms that are "deal-breakers" for you

- ☒ Once terms are agreed upon and the contract signed or proposal approved, you'll almost always need to sign a non-disclosure agreement (NDA) if you will be writing a novel

- ☒ Once the contract is signed or the job terms are agreed upon, send a follow-up note thanking your client

Workflow Process

- ☒ Create an outline and character writeups using whatever method works for you. I use Hiveword for this.

- ☒ Get the client's approval of the outline

- ☒ Make changes if necessary, based upon their input

- ☒ Set up a separate document for each book chapter or segment, using Google Docs and Drive or Microsoft Word and DropBox

- ☒ Suggestion: Set each file's name to Client-ChX-v1, where Client is the client's name and X is the number of the chapter.

- ☒ Set font to Times New Roman or Courier New, 12pt. Set page settings to 1" page margins and

1.5 line spacing. Make sure there is no space set between paragraphs.

☒ Write, keeping up with that plan's required daily WORDCOUNT.

☒ Complete draft of Chapter 1

☒ Complete draft of Chapter 2

☒ Make a copy of Chapter 1 and put copy in Archive folder

☒ Change version number to v2 on the Chapter 1 file

☒ Revise and self-edit Chapter 1

☒ Send revised Chapter 1 to the client, and begin Chapter 3 draft

---

☒ If the client then wants to see revisions to Chapter 1, tell him it will be revised after you've completed drafting the novel, so that you can be sure to meet your deadline. Whether you wait until later or find the time sooner is up to you. Clients love sooner.

- ☒ Always turn on Track Changes (Microsoft Word) or Suggestions (Google Docs) when inputting client requested revisions

- ☒ Repeat this process throughout the book, so that you're always editing and revising the chapter that came two chapters before the one you are currently writing.

- ☒ I write in Google Docs via Google Drive.

  - ○ When done, I rightclick the file and select Download. It auto-converts to MS Word.

  - ○ Then I email that file to the client, or post it to the jobs section if working through a content mill.

  - ○ When they send a document back to me, I drag-and-drop that into Google Drive, online, which auto-converts it to Google Docs format.

  - ○ Then in Google Drive, I rename the new file to match the old one, but I increase the number at the end of the filename. For example, "Smith-Ch1-v1" becomes "Smith-Ch1-v2".

○ I then only work on v2. In this way, you have a complete record of every version of every chapter, in addition to Google Docs' version history function.

⊠ Be sure to send your client a "quick update" email every week

Billing

⊠ If the client is working with you through a content mill, then billing is done through the mill as well

○ Remember to have the client *fund escrow* for the *next* segment, if you are working via milestones as I suggest

○ If working all on completion, which you may choose to do for small gigs with well-known clients, ensure at least half that amount is in escrow while you work so that you won't get scammed for all of it

○ If you are working for half up front and half on completion, ensure you get paid half upfront, and ensure the other half is placed in escrow *prior* to turning in the completed work—and make sure the client knows at the start that these are the terms

- ☒ If the client is working with you directly, rather than via a content mill, then log into PayPal

  - ○ Create an invoice for the *entire contract amount*

  - ○ Click the box on the invoice screen that allows you to "permit partial payments"

  - ○ The minimum payment amount you enter will be the total price divided by the number of milestones

  - ○ The client should put each milestone in escrow before you begin

Conclusion

- ☒ Once your client has accepted your submitted work, you are done with the project!

- ☒ Double-check that all payments have been made, just to be sure

- ☒ Thank your client for choosing you

- ☒ If they were easy to work with, invite them to contact you for another project in the future

- ☒ Lastly, ask for a rating and a review on the content mill, or on your Facebook Page or website, whichever is appropriate

- ☒ If using a content mill, remember to transfer released funds to your PayPal account, or you won't be able to spend it!

Taxes

At the end of the year, you'll need to file taxes. You may have the knowledge to file them correctly yourself, unlike me. I'm not an accountant or tax lawyer, so I recommend spending the extra bit of money to have a tax service prepare your returns.

Consider hiring an "Enrolled Agent," who is someone licensed by the IRS to practice tax law before the IRS as though they were a tax attorney. They are seldom much more expensive than a tax service, they spend enormous amounts of time and money staying current on tax law, and they often translate into getting more deductions, as well as a professional who will defend the deduction in tax court if you are ever audited.

Gather Paperwork and Receipts

Before going to see your tax preparer, you'll need to go to PayPal and print out a list of all money coming in, sorted by source. Draw a line through any transfers to PayPal that come from your bank account. Those are loans, i.e. debts, not income.

Likewise, print a list of all money going out, sorted by target. You may have hired professional services. You might have had to purchase software or hardware.

Perhaps you've had to buy magazines for research or because they relate to your business.

Draw a line through any money you transfer out of PayPal into your personal bank accounts. Those are draws, not expenses. (But talk to your tax preparer about how to handle those draws to report correctly to the IRS.)

Finally, print a list of PayPal fees you've paid. Often, when you receive money from a client, PayPal takes a very small amount as a fee. You can expense those Paypal fees.

Also, if you used a content mill such as Upwork to get gigs, you'll need to log in and print out your list of financial transactions. All fees from Upwork, PeoplePerHour or other job sites are business expenses.

When you're finished, you will have a full list of all business income and business expenses, sorted by source or target. If you used cash, personal checks, or personal credit cards for anything work-related, keep those receipts and bring them to the tax preparer along with your PayPal printouts.

Things to Deduct

Deductions must be logged and receipts kept in order to itemize them on your taxes. But what things are deductions? I've already mentioned content mill fees and PayPal fees, but other common deductions include:

- Stamps or postage

- Stationary and other business supplies

- Computers, printers, printer ink, cell phones and service, other electronics you use for your business

- Bank account fees for any professional bank account that you use to receive PayPal transfers

- Advertising expenses for your business, including social media promotions

- Google Drive extra storage, if you pay for it

- Any domain name or site hosting expenses

- Your internet bill

- Website or organization membership fees, if they relate in any way to your business, such as for research or for networking

- Magazine subscriptions and cost of books purchased, so long as they relate either to your business, to writing, or to a topic you are writing about. For example, if you purchase a nonfiction atlas of Civil War battles, and you ghostwrite a Civil War-era romance novel, that book is a business expense and is deductible.

- Some portion of your power and/or natural gas bill

- Office rent, if you rent a separate office space. If you work from a home office, you'll need to talk to a tax expert to determine if you can or should claim a home office deduction.

Again, I'm not an accountant or tax attorney. Talk to your tax preparer about these deductions and any others that may apply.

I strongly recommend you do not try to prepare your business tax papers yourself. The potential price tag of making tax filing mistakes is far too high to take that risk, in my opinion.

Closing

Getting into ghostwriting can seem daunting. Because so few know about this field, there are even fewer books that discuss the nuts-and-bolts techniques you need to begin, grow, and thrive as a ghostwriting professional.

My goal with this book has been to enable you to launch your own ghostwriting business (or side business); show the ethics of ghostwriting and explain the kinds of ghostwriting contracts available; help you get new clients and build your portfolio; and ultimately, to use ghostwriting as a means to an end. That end goal is to improve your own writing so you can launch your *own books*, and use ghostwriting to fund things like editors and book covers.

You'll need all these things to succeed, but if you follow the steps and do the work, approach it ethically and professionally, and stay motivated, success can be yours. Will be yours.

After reading this book, I think you can sense intuitively that it works. The steps make sense, right? If I can do this, you can, too!

All this book's links and many more are available

through a hidden page on my website, which I've created just for you. It's my way of saying thank you for reading my book! Simply go to http://smarturl.it/GWritingResources. Thanks!

Appendix: Samples

Content Mill Proposal

The key, in my experience, is to sound both professional and approachable. In other words, someone who is a joy to work with professionally. Note how I assume he's going to hire me. Always do that! I also keep it short, but it's longer than many of the proposals they get.

Feel free to take my example proposal and modify it for your own needs.

Dear Mike,

Thank you for taking time to review my proposal [Or for inviting you to submit one, if that's the case], because I'm very interested in ghostwriting your 50k-word scifi novel. You'll find me diligent, thorough, and above all, easy to work with. My number-one goal is to get a 5-star review from you, and earn it. I intend to be your first choice for the next book, as well!

If selected for this project, your listed deadline of MM/DD/YYYY will be no problem. Will you be providing me with an outline, or a summary? My attached bid assumes you will, but I'm flexible on price—I'm sure I can meet your budget needs, as well as your deadline.

Thanks again for reviewing this. I look forward to working with you!

Sincerely,

Yourname Goeshere

Email Proposal

The email proposal requires a bit more bravery, and more length, but it's an ideal opportunity to gain a reference, portfolio item, and maybe even a co-author credit. You still wouldn't get royalties, unless you negotiate for that instead of an upfront fee, but it's an actual credit that will help you later when you write and publish your own novels!

You need to get creative, but it can be fun to look for people who might be interested in an autobiography, website content, blog posts, etc. Here's an example email that pitches a local businessman with the idea of an autobiography (which you will write, of course).

Dear Peter,

I noticed from your advertisement that you've been an entrepreneur in Atlanta for twenty years, and that's impressive. Yet, you don't have a book out, I noticed. I'd like to talk to you about maybe collaborating on an autobiography, detailing your inspiring history in the area. Is this something you've considered before?

I found a similar autobiography from another businessman in Charlotte, NC. It was published five years ago, yet it remains in the top 1000 on Amazon for its genre. That means over 5,275* people have bought his book and that's a whole lot of credibility! [* **Note:** *Determined by going to* _https://goo.gl/mZBa1u_ and entering a competitor's book information; multiply the result x years since it was published x 365. It's not perfect, but close enough.]

If this seems like a project for which you would be interested in working with a professional writer, I'd love to talk more about how we can work together to write your own autobiography. Maybe we could talk over coffee? My treat.

I look forward to hearing from you,

Yourname Goeshere

Letter of Understanding

As I've said in this book, I greatly prefer the Letter of Understanding/Memo of Understanding. I try to avoid contracts where possible, because they always disadvantage _you_, not the client, it seems. You also need an attorney to make sure the agreement actually means what you think it means, since in legal terms, things often mean something other than the common

English understanding of those words' meaning. The letter is long, but pretty comprehensive. It favors you, so long as your requirements are clearly stated.

January 3, 2017

Dear Mr. Smith:

According to our prior messenger conversation, I have agreed to ghostwrite your 80,000-word scifi novel. All communications regarding this manuscript will be conducted via email or messenger, or as we both may agree in the future. I have received a copy of the outline from you via email, downloaded it, and this is the outline version that I will write to unless you say otherwise.

I have agreed on this occasion to provide ghostwriting services for a discounted total rate of $800. Each word over the estimated 80,000 words will be written at a rate of $0.02/word, and I agree to discuss any such work with you before beginning. As we discussed, In your estimation, the book will take 15 days to complete. However, I've gone over the project and find I'll need 39 days from the date I begin writing. This letter of understanding is contingent upon your agreement to this new timeline and adjusted deadline.

We will have eight (8) milestones, each 10,000 words in length, with the first milestone payable in advance. At each milestone's completion, payment will be due for the subsequent milestone, which must be paid in full before the next milestone's content will be delivered.

If additional words over the originally envisioned 80,000 are required and agreed to, payment for such content will be due upon completion and delivery of the additional content needed, unless the additional words total more than 10,000 words. At 10,000 additional words, and for each additional 10,000 words, payment is due for the prior *segment before the next segment will be delivered.*

I include one 15-minute conference call per week to discuss the project. Additional calls, or additional time, are payable at $40/hour with a 1/4-hour minimum.

I understand that this is work-for-hire and no employee/employer relationship exists. I understand that all content written will belong solely to you, upon payment for that content. I will receive no royalties for this work, nor any copyright or other ownership rights. Furthermore, I agree to be bound by the terms of our non-disclosure agreement, whether verbal or written; I will not discuss with any outside party either the work being done or your identity, without prior written authorization from you.

You agree that no non-compete agreement exists. This letter of understanding supersedes all other written documents, signed or not, whether prior, current, or in the future. I am free to pursue other ghostwriting/writing work, in any genre, at any time.

I will need to know by Thursday, January 5, whether you intend to proceed. At that time, should either of us decide not to continue with the project, no compensation will be due.

Upon your acceptance of the terms of this letter of understanding, I will deliver to you an invoice for the full amount via PayPal, which will permit payment of less than the full amount but with a minimum payment that corresponds to the agreed upon rate. My usual practice is to apply interest if payment is not made within 30 days, at an interest rate of 2% per month or partial month beyond 30 days. If you terminate our agreement after work has begun, I will be paid a prorated amount based on the portion of the manuscript already written at the time notice is received, and an additional cancellation fee of $200, to be paid before current-milestone content will be delivered.

Should you decide after the job is completed that you would like the manuscript to undergo a second stage of revision writing, that work will be the subject of a separate agreement.

However, I am happy to provide you with a complimentary bonus service we did not discuss: light revisions of each milestone I deliver to you, if such revisions are requested within 30 days of that milestone's delivery to you. I simply feel it's something I would want from my writer if our roles were reversed, so I'm providing it to you at no additional fee.

The purpose of this complementary revision will be to "polish" the material and incorporate any changes you make with track-changes on. Such changes may not account more than 5% of the milestone's total word count, or in this case an editing/revising up to 500 words revised. Revisions over 500 edited words, or over the milestone's original wordcount, are subject to a separate agreement and are not included in this letter of understanding.

If you agree to the terms of this letter of understanding, please respond to this email with a statement to that effect. I will then send the project invoice and await payment of the initial installment, at which point writing will begin. I don't foresee any other expenses associated with this project and will inform you right away if I encounter any.

Thank you for your consideration. I appreciate your time and your trust with this manuscript. I understand it represents a significant personal investment, and I will treat it with the respect it and you deserve.

Sincerely,

Yourname Goeshere

About the Author

J.S. Menefee lives in eastern Washington. He has been a freelance writer/editor for over 20 years. He has ghostwritten a dozen novels and many nonfiction works, and is the author of *The Professional Ghostwriter's Handbook*. He is developing a Paranormal Urban Fantasy novel set, which he gleefully refers to as his "PUF" project.

You can follow him online at—

- **Amazon:** http://hyperurl.co/AmazonAuthor
- **Facebook Author Page:** http://hyperurl.co/JMFacebookPage
- **Facebook Freelancing Page:** http://smarturl.it/FBFreelancer
- **Author's Website:** http://hyperurl.co/jsmenefee
- **Freelancing Blog:** http://hyperurl.co/JMenefeeFreelance
- **Twitter:** @AuthorJSMenefee

Join my totally non-spammy newsletter!
http://smarturl.it/JSMNewsletter
Generally issued once monthly unless there's significant news, the newsletter includes cover reveals, new books, recommended reading, as well as giveaways and free content.

The end of this book isn't the end, because...

There's one last thing.

You bought my book, and so now, I want to give you a copy of another ebook!

Simply copy or click the link below and follow the directions, and I'll share it with you at no cost.

Simply to thank you for your time and buying my book!

Click Here:
3 Easy Outlines for Ghostwriters: Quickly ghostwrite novels that Rock!
(http://smarturl.it/3EasyOutlines_GWH)

67446154R00095

Made in the USA
Middletown, DE
11 September 2019